Endorse

Anita Rahma's book *Downward Discipleship* invites us to the lived reality of following Jesus by serving the poor and oppressed. The story is interwoven with that of Amy Carmichael who saved girls from prostitution in India last century. Anita has drawn from Amy's writing and woven it into her own journey of living in the slums of Jakarta, providing schooling for children, and grappling with suffering and poverty. She gives us glimpses of her own life with her responses of songs and personal reflection in the nitty gritty of life on the margins.

IRENE ALEXANDER, PhD
Asian Theological Seminary, Stillpoint, Brisbane,
Trinity College Queensland Honorary Research Fellow
Author, *Practicing the Presence of Jesus* and *How Relationships Work*

Planted deep inside the wounds of our world, Anita Rahma offers a testimony of hope and healing. Looking through the lens of nineteenth-century missionary Amy Carmichael, we are afforded a perspective on the many "whys" that surround the lives of those who are suffering. In the end, we shift our focus from the why, and turn our attention to the Who that walks among the marginalized.

SCOTT BESSENECKER
Global Engagement & Justice, InterVarsity Christian Fellowship
Author, *The New Friars* and *How to Inherit the Earth*

Reading *Downward Discipleship* is like joining author Anita Rahma and legendary missionary Amy Carmichael to share stories over a cup of tea! In the book, Rahma gently but firmly invites the reader to embrace seven different paradigm shifts. In the process, Rahma outlines a vision for Christian discipleship that follows Jesus to the cultural and social margins. Whether you are serving in or with a disadvantaged community or not, *Downward Discipleship* will help you live a life of joyful and purposeful surrender in your life of faith.

ROB DIXON, DIS
Author, *Together in Ministry: Women and Men in Flourishing Partnerships*

By interweaving the story of legendary missionary, Amy Carmichael, with her own journey to the slums of Indonesia, Rahma offers us a front row seat to a life lived with purpose. But the goal is not to place yet another hero on yet another pedestal. Instead, this is an invitation for *all* of us to be deeply transformed. These are lessons that can only be learned on the margins of society, among the poor. Read and be challenged.

CRAIG GREENFIELD
Founder, Alongsiders International
Author, *Subversive Mission*

Across the global pain of two billion urban poor, there are multiplying movements inspired by Christ, the suffering servant, to live among them. Anita dearly represents the multiple levels of the struggles to find an understanding of the depths of spirituality amidst such struggles. Her authorship is unique in its ability to integrate the complexities yet identify the singularities of action. Some books drive you deeper towards the living God—read them—read this one!

VIV GRIGG, PhD

Author, *Companion to the Poor, Cry of the Urban Poor, Spirit of Christ and the Postmodern City, Kiwinomics, SlumDwellers' Pedagogy*

The unique approach in Anita Rahma's second book is to learn from and then engage the reader with the life of Amy Carmichael, a missionary in India one hundred years before Anita was called to downward discipleship. Building on her first book, *Beyond Our Walls: Finding Jesus in the Slums of Jakarta*, Anita Rahma takes her readers deeper into an exploration of the ever-present challenges and accompanying joy and contentment that comes with following Jesus into the suffering of the world. Anita points out that Jesus sought out the lowest in his culture and did not live as one with privilege even though he was Lord of all creation. We are all called to downward discipleship rather than upward mobility, though not all may be called to the same locations and lifestyles. Some readers will be challenged to leave comfort behind and to find the courage, as Anita has, through giants of faith who have gone before to live an incarnational life of chosen poverty. Perhaps others will be confronted with the need to live more thoughtfully and be used by God to support the Anita's and Amy's in the world. Each chapter introduces the downward discipleship topic such as "from control to compassion," asks a related question of Amy's life and shares a situation in Anita's own life. Bringing Amy Carmichael's life to the reader deepens our connection with those who, through the ages, have lived for God by serving others.

In every age there are those who hear and respond to the call to love and serve in the world's hardest places. May we read this book with an open heart and prayerful spirit, ready to respond to God's call for us, and comforted by God's faithful care and leading along that path.

ANN GRABER HERSHBERGER, PhD

Emeritus Professor of Nursing, Eastern Mennonite University

Executive Director, Mennonite Central Committee

In Anita Rahma's *Downward Discipleship*, one reads many Biblical insights as she focuses on the importance of a deeper relationship with God. The reader finds theology not from the desk but from the kitchen table. Working for so many years for those at the edge of society, Anita sees with the eyes as Jesus saw the needy and the broken-hearted. I share with Anita the ongoing inspiration from the work of Amy Carmichael in Dohnavur in India. Triggered by the deep insights from this God-fearing woman who started her work in the outgoing Victorian era, the author found beautiful gems to implement these in her work in the slums of Jakarta. Spiritually charged throughout, this book is written with passion and compassion. Vigorous reflections thoughtfully drawn from Amy Carmichael's writings and skillfully presented, underline Rahma's thoughts about doing missionary work amongst very vulnerable people. This book gives the reader insights into the practical challenges which missionary work encounters in areas away from mainstream city life. In the grim reality of the Jakarta slums we meet Christian devotedness and personal faith in God.

J. KOMMERS, PhD
North-West University (NWU), Potchefstroom, South Africa
Author, *Triumphant Love: The Contextual, Creative and Strategic Missionary Work of Amy Beatrice Carmichael in South India*

Inspiring. Chock-full of wisdom. And potentially life-changing. In *Downward Discipleship*, Anita Rahma calls her readers to set aside their comfort and follow Jesus on his long, purposeful descent to the bottom of society. Woven throughout this book, Rahma shares personal stories from her mission work among the urban poor while also introducing us to one of her spiritual heroes—an early twentieth-century missionary to India named Amy Carmichael. For nearly fifty years, Carmichael worked tirelessly to rescue temple children from forced prostitution and slave-like conditions. Her life and writings have deeply impacted Rahma's own sense of call, as I pray Rahma's life and writings will now do for you.

JASON PORTERFIELD
Author, *Fight Like Jesus*

Why did Amy Carmichael do what she did? If you are one who wants to deeply understand and emulate her model of selfless service, this is the book. Amy's unshakeable faith in both the transcendent and Immanent nature of God is clearly evident in acknowledging due reverence and also constant presence of the divine in every aspect of her life. Rahma has found writings and stories from Amy's life and connected it to her own life to learn to face fear and overcome guilt, slowly giving up control and surrender to God—shunning worldly temptations and drawing comfort and strength in her own struggles. Her quotes from Amy in the beginning of each chapter are perfect and real, and it showed how much she's been deeply affected and touched by Amy's life and writings. It is very comforting to know that everything that Amy wrote as her own questions and struggles has found deep meaning in the life of another woman living in a different culture, place, and time. This is a practical manual on serving others filled by divine love.

JEREMIAH RAJANESAN
CEO, The Dohnavur Fellowship, South India

The author combines her personal journey downward with quotes and insights from Amy Carmichael who, over a century earlier, had served among the poor of India for over fifty years of her life. This book is a powerful invitation to spread beauty through the world. In poetry and prose, in accounts of personal struggle and freedom from control, fear, and self-gratification, reading the Bible in a garbage dump gives Rahma the perspective of a downward disciple, who like Jesus, descended to live with those below the lines of poverty, injustice, and thoughtless privilege and easy abundance. At once prophetic and inspiring, *Downward Discipleship* is a refreshing cross-centered, cross-cultural, counter-cultural example of two women who embody the good news of Jesus authentically. The story of Amy and Rahma will change your perspective, and potentially, your life.

LINFORD STUTZMAN, PHD
Emeritus Professor of Culture, Religion and Mission, Eastern Mennonite University
Author, *Sailing Acts* and *With Paul at Sea*

In Anita Rahma's usual fashion, *Downward Discipleship* delivers truth from unexpected angles. Her thoughtful reflections on blessing and privilege and the way Western workers often feel guilt over their own privilege spoke deeply to me. Her stories of walking with God and walking with the poor inspired me to be more of a spiritual doula with the people in my life—patiently walking with them and allowing God, not me, to do the transforming.

ELIZABETH TROTTER
Editor-in-chief, *A Life Overseas* (missions website)
Co-author, *Serving Well*

DOWNWARD DISCIPLESHIP

How Amy Carmichael Gave Me Courage to Serve in a Slum

By Anita Rahma

WILLIAM CAREY PUBLISHING

Available at missionbooks.org

Published by William Carey Publishing
10 W. Dry Creek Cir
Littleton, CO 80120 | www.missionbooks.org

William Carey Publishing is a ministry of Frontier Ventures
Pasadena, CA | www.frontierventures.org

Cover and Interior Designer: Mike Riester
Cover image is a composit of an image from freepix.com and a public domain image of Amy Carmichael serving in India.

ISBNs: 978-1-64508-552-2 (paperback)
       978-1-64508-554-6 (epub)

Printed Worldwide

28 27 26 25 24   1 2 3 4 5   IN

Library of Congress Control Number: 2024930179

To Yosiah, my husband,
the love of my life and my best friend.
I am forever grateful to be on this journey
together!

Often I wonder...
where in the history of our religion
we first dropped the painful Cross,
and forgot to go back for it.

—Amy Carmichael, *From the Forest*[1]

1 Carmichael, *From the Forest*, Kindle ed., 1647.

Contents

Prologue   xiii

Invitation 1: *From Fear to Friendship*   1
    Asking Amy: *How do we sing in the night?*
    Seeing Fears Transformed by Friendships
    Encountering Jesus in Places of Addiction
    Room to Reflect

Invitation 2: *From Self to Surrender*   19
    Asking Amy: *How can we find peace?*
    Surrendering to God's Timing
    Surrendering to a Lifetime of Learning
    Room to Reflect

Invitation 3: *From Guilt to Gratitude*   31
    Asking Amy: *How can our lives overflow with gratitude?*
    Living in Paradox
    Finding Jesus in Surprising Places
    Room to Reflect

Invitation 4: *From Control to Compassion*   41
    Asking Amy: *What can we do when we feel helpless and out of control?*
    Trusting God When We Cannot See
    Bringing Our Laments to the Lord
    Room to Reflect

Invitation 5: *From Mammon to Manna*   53
    Asking Amy: *How will the Lord provide?*
    Giving More than Money
    Trusting God in Times of Scarcity and Plenty
    Room to Reflect

Invitation 6: *From Poverty to Praise*   65
    Asking Amy: *How can we be sustained through seasons of suffering?*
    Clinging to Christ's Hope in Times of Disappointment
    Discerning the Sacred Task of the Doula
    Room to Reflect

Invitation 7: *From Asking Why? to Welcoming the Word*   75
    Asking Amy: *What can we do with our questions?*
    Recognizing We Need a Savior
    Rooting Ourselves in God's Word
    Room to Reflect

Conclusion   85
Epilogue   89
Appendix A: Journal Entry   91
Appendix B: Songs   93
Acknowledgments   99
Bibliography   101

Prologue

Sooner or later we must all come to the place where we hear a voice—a voice that is deep with unfathomable pain—calling us to the fellowship of suffering. But there we find Him. And who but Jesus—the crucified, risen Redeemer—could suffice us there?

—Amy Carmichael, *Mimosa*[1]

Several years ago, my son and I were walking home after visiting his best friend in our slum community. During the dry season, that walk could take five minutes, but during the rainy season, this walk with my three-year-old son could take almost thirty minutes. We were both wearing "gum boots," as our New Zealand friends call them, as we carefully trudged through sticky mud and wet, stinky garbage. My one-year-old son was tied to me with the traditional batik fabric Indonesian women use to carry their babies. Suddenly my eldest let go of my hand and stomped ahead, then tripped and fell face down in the filthy mud.

"I don't need a bath! I don't need a bath," he started screaming over and over again.

I tried not to think of the chemicals that might be mixed in with the oozing mud covering his face, shirt, and pants as we hurried home, with him still screaming. He did get a bath!

This somewhat traumatic experience left a lasting impression on me. A lot of times, I act like my three-year-old. I fall down, make mistakes, but my pride gets in the way of acknowledging my need for help. I might be a complete mess, but I keep screaming to God and whoever might listen, "I don't need a bath. I can do it myself. I'm fine!"

This often seems to be the case for the whole church as well. We like to pretend that everything is beautiful, even when we are covered in garbage.

Will I let Jesus wash me?

Will we let Jesus cleanse us?

During this season in my life, I was slowly emerging from years of "young motherhood fog," trying desperately to survive and hold onto hope by listening to podcasts and reading books in snippets when I had enough mental energy. While working my way through recordings of several Urbana seminars,[2] I was drawn to one in particular, "Women in the World Mission:

---

1 Carmichael, *Mimosa*, Kindle ed., 1542.

2 The Urbana Missions Convention normally occurs every three years. Recordings of many seminars can be found at urbana.org for several years after each event.

The Untold Story."[3] Ironically, this one-hour seminar was taught by a man, Rob Dixon, but I am forever grateful for the way it expanded my knowledge and gave me helpful direction to continue learning on my own. One of the recommended books that Dixon mentioned was *50 Women Every Christian Should Know* by Michelle DeRusha, which introduced me to forty-three women I had never heard of before. This seems humbling to admit, as I had grown up in a Christian home and majored in "missions" in university.

While each of the fifty women mentioned in the book have compelling stories, Amy Carmichael captured my curiosity. I had only ever heard her name in relation to the quote: "I don't wonder apostolic miracles have died. Apostolic living certainly has."[4] Wanting to learn more about her life, I got a copy of Elisabeth Elliot's *A Chance to Die: The Life and Legacy of Amy Carmichael.* As I dove into Elliot's beautiful biography, I was amazed by Amy's legacy, as she wrote countless books during her years of ministry that are still available for us to read over a century later.

What draws me to this fiery Irish missionary, who left her home, sailed to India, and never returned? What relevance does Amy's story have for Christians living in the twenty-first century? Why did I pour myself into book after book written by or about Amy Carmichael?

Downward Discipleship is my attempt to answer these questions and to share how Amy's story has impacted my own. As I have lived and served in an urban slum community in Indonesia for more than ten years, her writings from rural India have resonated across the ocean and more than a century, encouraging me to follow Jesus by coming down from my North American pedestal of self-obsession so that I might seek Christ and his kingdom, where the last will be first and the first will be last (Matt 20:16). Rather than seeking after a path of "upward mobility" toward a comfortable middle-class existence, with a guaranteed retirement plan and scheduled daily devotional hour, Amy has helped me focus on *following* the example of Jesus, who sought out those in the lowest position of his culture. Jesus *stooped* to wash his disciples' feet (John 13:1–5) and instructed his followers to imitate his example (vv. 14–15). Jesus *picked up his cross* (John 19:17) and invites us to pick up our own crosses and follow him on a daily journey of sacrifice (Matt 16:24). Amy has helped me see that even though the life of following

> What draws me to this fiery Irish missionary, who left her home, sailed to India, and never returned?

---

3 Dixon, "Women in the World Mission."

4 Quoted by Hayes, "Incarnational Ministry in Four Dimensions."

Jesus may not include abundant possessions, it will include abundant love, meaning, purpose, and a living relationship with Jesus.

Amy's message—lived through the example of her life and vividly captured in her beautiful writings—calls us to follow Christ to the margins by embracing a life of downward discipleship.

Many of the stories from my own journey are already recorded in my first book *Beyond Our Walls: Finding Jesus in the Slums of Jakarta*. In *Downward Discipleship*, I weave new stories together with quotes and stories from Amy Carmichael's life and ministry. All the names in the stories have been changed due to security reasons. Most twenty-first-century Christians are not going to sit down and read Amy's books, as the English can be archaic and difficult to understand, but I believe that her story continues to be relevant to us today. Mother Teresa has remained internationally famous long after her death, and I believe that Amy should be regarded as a Protestant Mother Teresa—a heroine of the faith—and yet many Christians today have never heard her name.

I hope that my humble attempt to share her story will spark your curiosity to read more and inspire you to begin—or to continue—your own journey of downward discipleship.

As Amy writes: "Life is full, there is hardly time to live, much less to set down all that is in it. Still, sometimes such episodes are distinct in emphasis, and looking back we remember the years of the right hand of the Most High, and are reinforced in faith."[5] My prayer is that this book might help you remember the "years of the right hand of the Most High" in your life, and in remembering, may your faith be reinforced and your hope enlivened.

---

5 Carmichael, *Nor Scrip*, Kindle ed., 1787.

Invitation 1

From Fear to Friendship

We take courage again, and ask forgiveness for our fears. It is true our problems are not always solved, and perhaps more difficult days are before; but we will not be afraid. Sometimes a sudden light falls on the way, and we look up and still it shines: and what can we do but "follow the Gleam"?

—Amy Carmichael, *Lotus Buds*[1]

Be still, for I am with you. Peace, my child, do not fear.
I am your rock of refuge, your firm foundation, your rock of safety.
You may be shaken, but I'm firmly beneath your feet.
I am your brother's keeper.

—Journal entry, January 2011

Fear is a common human emotion, and yet Scripture is filled with the invitation to move beyond fear to something else entirely. Followers of Christ are called to surrender our fears and choose to trust in the One who holds the whole world in his hands. Often, our journeys of faith may start with being afraid—afraid of hell, afraid of failure, afraid of disappointing our Savior, and our endless list of fears could go on. But I believe God wants to call us beyond these fears into friendship with God as well as friendship with the people we serve. We are invited to let love—love for the Lord and love from God for others—transform our lives.

From Amy Carmichael, we learn that her life was not without fear. She was afraid of many things, both spiritually and physically, during her long life of service. However, her friendship with the Lord changed everything, for Jesus was her guide and Lord, her lover and her faithful companion through the ups and downs of the half-century she served in India.

When we choose to follow Jesus by stepping down from our pedestals of power and prestige and offering our lives in service of his kingdom, we will find ourselves in intense situations that will require great faith and courage. Will we be bound by our fears? Or will we release our fears as we choose to place our trust in a loving God, who promises to journey with us as we walk through the valley of the shadow of death (Ps 23:4)? In times of darkness and confusion, how can we continue to choose friendship with the Lord?

---

1 Carmichael, *Lotus Buds*, Kindle ed., 834.

Asking Amy: *How do we sing in the night?*[2]

And as for older travellers whom Love has led over hill and dale, they have not been given the spirit of fear. They think of the way they have come since they stood on that bright hillside, and their word is always this: There are reasons and reasons for hope and for happiness, and never one for fear....Even though we must walk in the land of fear, there is no need to fear. The power of His resurrection comes before the fellowship of His sufferings.

—Amy Carmichael, *Gold by Moonlight*[3]

Amy Beatrice Carmichael was born in Ireland on December 16, 1867, to parents of Scottish descent. They lived in a large stone house in the village of Millisle on the northern coast of Ireland.[4] Her parents raised Amy and her six siblings in the Presbyterian church, and faith was an integrated part of their family's life.

Amy had a happy childhood, enjoying horseback riding and explorations along the rocky beach near their house. Her father and uncle owned a flour mill business, as well as more than one hundred acres of land, and therefore Amy grew up in a wealthy and comfortable home. Her parents could afford to pay for private lessons during Amy's elementary school years. However, her world began to broaden when she spent three years at a Wesleyan Methodist boarding school in Yorkshire, England. She was no stranger to fear and after those three years away from home, financial strain on the family necessitated Amy returning to Ireland. Soon afterwards, her parents told her they would move from their family farm to the large city of Belfast. There were many fears pressing into her teenage mind—being uprooted from all that was familiar and starting somewhere new. Life in a small Irish village was replaced by the noisy, dirty streets of the city.

Then when Amy was eighteen, her father passed away, which launched her family into a time of grief and crisis. As the oldest of the seven siblings, Amy must have felt a huge emotional responsibility for her family's well-being, for soon after her father's death, they were plunged deeper into financial difficulties and eventually had to file for bankruptcy.

---

2 Unless otherwise noted, the information for this biographical sketch was taken from Elliot, *Chance to Die*; Kommers, *Triumphant Love*; the Heroes of the Faith documentary, *Amy Carmichael: Mother to the Motherless*, as well as information gleaned from reading the extensive list of Amy's writings listed in the bibliography.

3 Carmichael, *Gold by Moonlight*, 15–16.

4 Now part of Northern Ireland.

Yet Amy did not let the fears of her new surroundings and unfortunate circumstances paralyze her. Instead, she embraced her new situation as an opportunity to learn and serve those around her. Amy had given her life to Christ while at boarding school, and she believed that God's love needed to be shared with others. While many people are afraid of those who are different, Amy began to befriend the young women who worked long days in the mills of Belfast. These girls were known as the "shawlies," because they could not afford hats and instead covered their hair with shawls. Amy ignored the fears of the "respectable people" around her as she invested herself in reaching these young women through weekly Bible studies and inviting them to worship services.

> *Amy visited the Keswick Convention, where her heart was stirred for missions.*

As more of the women joined these services, Amy began to pray for a meeting space. In time, she convinced a nearby Mill to sell them a plot of land, and a generous woman donated funds for constructing a building that came to be known as "The Tin Tabernacle."[5] Later, this became the Welcome Evangelical Church, which still exists today.[6] The Tin Tabernacle was not just a place for worship, but also functioned as a community center, where youth could learn sewing, attend night school, and study the Bible.

A few years later, the family relocated to Manchester, England, where Amy was invited by a family friend to begin similar work. In Manchester, Amy lived in a slum area and learned about life with rats and cockroaches. She continued to reach out to young women working in factories until her health declined, and she was forced to take a break.

During this time, Amy visited the Keswick Convention,[7] where her heart was stirred for missions. Fear about her future was replaced with faith and conviction that one day she would serve overseas. She heard many visiting missionaries preach, including Hudson Taylor,[8] and she experienced her own deep call to share the gospel overseas. On January 13, 1892, she heard a voice in her ears say clearly, "Go ye." Although she wanted to go as soon

---

5 This was a large building made of tin that was constructed for 500 British pounds and was large enough to seat hundreds of people.

6 Welcome Evangelical Church, "Amy Carmichael Centre."

7 The Keswick Convention began in 1875 and continues today. Formerly for one week each summer, now for three weeks, the Keswick Convention draws thousands of Christians from the UK and around the world to gather for worship, prayer, and inspiration. Kommers, *Triumphant Love*, Kindle ed., 174.

8 Hudson Taylor (1832–1905) was a missionary to China and founded the China Inland Mission. He spent over fifty years in China and inspired a movement of missionaries.

as possible, she grieved the thought of leaving loved ones behind (including her mother and her adoptive father, Mr. Wilson, cofounder of the Keswick Convention).

Amy suffered from neuralgia, and this painful nerve disease sometimes forced her to bed for weeks at a time. Initially, it seemed her poor health might prevent her from going overseas, but eventually she was sent as a Keswick missionary and boarded a ship to sail to Japan when she was twenty-five years old. As she said goodbye to her family, her heart broke. More than fifty years later, Amy reflected:

> Never, I think, not even in Heaven shall I forget that parting.... It was such a rending thing that I never wanted to repeat it.... Even now my heart winces at the thought of it....The night I sailed for China, March 3, 1893, my life, on the human side, was broken, and it never was mended again. But *He has been enough.*[9]

After one year in Japan,[10] she relocated to Sri Lanka for her health and then soon after returned to England to visit loved ones. It seemed like doors were closing for her, but she would not be deterred. After a ten-month rest, she set sail for India on October 11, 1895—never to return to England. Amy arrived in India in November, extremely sick with dengue fever. A friend had invited her to join a mission in Bangalore, a city in South India with an elevation of three thousand feet.

Amy began by focusing on language and culture learning, finding Tamil extremely difficult. A note in her Bible, next to Psalm 34:4 states, "September 1896. Fears. Fears of failure. Fears of future. All my fears. There is a balm for every pain, a medicine for all sorrow. The eye turned backward to the Cross and forward to the morrow. The morrow of the glory."[11] After more than a year of learning, Mr. and Mrs. Walker, missionaries who had been in India for ten years, invited Amy to join them in starting itinerating work.[12] In February of 1897, Amy received a "yes" from God and began the harrowing ministry of traveling to different towns to share the gospel. Mr. and Mrs. Walker became invaluable friends and mentors for Amy as she tried to find her feet in India.

As Amy and the Walkers worked together in the south of India, they longed to reach those of high castes. In the late 1800s and early 1900s, the caste system

---

9 Elliot, *Chance to Die*, 64.

10 To read about Amy's experiences in Japan, see Carmichael, *From Sunrise Land.*

11 Quoted by Kommers, *Triumphant Love*, Kindle ed., 367.

12 "Itinerating" refers to traveling from village to village, sharing the gospel. They stayed in tents and travelled by bullock bandy.

was still practiced throughout India. While there were Christian converts from "lower" castes, the Brahman communities (the highest-ranking caste group) were often without a single convert. The cultural laws and practices meant that she literally could not touch those she was trying to reach, as she would "defile them." Years of itinerating seemed to bring little fruit. When there were the rare occurrences of Hindus showing interest in Christ or choosing to believe, they often came to

> *The cultural laws and practices meant that Amy literally could not touch those she was trying to reach, as she would "defile them."*

tragic ends—tortured, poisoned, forced into early marriages, imprisoned in homes, and even killed.

But year after year, Amy and her team of Western and Indian coworkers labored on. Visiting village after village, festival after festival, home after home, they shared about Christ through songs, poems, stories, and conversations. Amy knew what it was like to have entire villages close their doors to her, and there were times of intense rejection and real danger. She was no stranger to having dust and rocks thrown at her. Yet she also knew the intense joy of seeing hungry people taste of Christ's goodness, along with the beauty of seeing people transformed by God's forgiveness and then extending forgiveness to others.

Amy was also not afraid to combat larger systems of evil. While she did not realize it at the time, a few years into her service in southern India, something happened that would shape the direction of her future ministry. Early in the morning on March 6, 1901,[13] Amy was reading on her veranda when she saw a child approaching her, accompanied by an Indian Christian woman from a nearby village. The child, who was about seven years old, had shown up the evening before at the woman's house, asking to be brought to the missionaries.

Recalling this incident, Amy writes: "'My name is Pearl-eyes,' the child began, 'and I want to stay here always. I have come to stay.' And she told us how her mother had sold her when she was a baby to the Servants of the gods. She was not happy with them. They did not love her. Nobody loved her. She wanted to live with us."[14]

This introduced Amy to the journey that she would give the rest of her life to: fighting to rescue children from being "married to the gods." While most foreigners turned a blind eye to this reality in India, Amy began to

---

13 Carmichael, *Beginning of a Story*, Kindle ed., 742.
14 Carmichael, *Things as They Are*, Kindle ed., 415.

learn about the hidden world of temples. Young girls (as well as boys) were given as infants or as young children to the temples and would spend their lives serving in the temples. In many cases, this included molestation and prostitution as part of worship.

> The practice involved grooming girls, some of them only babies, for a life of ritualised prostitution. These girls were a valuable commodity since they would become the sex slaves of the Brahman priests who ran the temples. Considered as property of the gods, the girls had no rights of their own and could be sexually abused and tortured without censure. Parents giving children to the temple were taught it was meritorious and since there were often financial rewards to the parents who did so, many children were—even before birth—dedicated to the temple.[15]

After Pearl-eyes joined Amy and her team, it was three years before a second temple child was brought to them.[16]

Amy writes, "In the autumn of 1903, when my comrades, Mr. and Mrs. Walker, had to go to England, I was much alone with the Lord Jesus. It was then that the burden of the little Temple children pressed so heavily that I could not bear it any longer—'Lord, what wilt Thou have me to do?' I asked, and the answer came quite clearly: 'Search for the little lost lambs with Me.' And so the work began."[17] Eventually, Amy and her band of women gave up their itinerating work to make a home for the children that they rescued.[18]

There were many things to fear: government lawsuits, angry temple women, violent relatives. But Amy and her coworkers carried on—amidst incredible opposition—and eventually founded the Dohnavur Fellowship, which became home to hundreds of children. Over the years, it expanded to include a school and a hospital and has touched thousands of lives.

Over the fifty-six years that Amy spent in India, she faced many challenges and terrifying experiences.

In *The Beginning of a Story*, Amy explains: "We did not choose Dohnavur. We were living here, itinerating in the country round, an almost entirely Hindu tract, with many wholly Hindu towns and villages scattered about upon it, when the

---

15 Kommers, *Triumphant Love*, Kindle ed., 369. Girls who were "married to the gods" became "temple women," also known as *Devadasis*.

16 "On March 1, 1904, the first temple baby, thirteen days old, was in Amma's arms." Elliot, *Chance to Die*, 182.

17 Carmichael, *Beginning of a Story*, Kindle ed., 742.

18 By 1904, Amy had made her home in Dohnavur and was caring for seventeen children. Kommers, *Triumphant Love*, Kindle ed., 417.

work for the little children grew up about us, and before we knew it, we were a family."[19] Dohnavur proved to be the perfect location to sink down roots, and it was where Amy spent the rest of her life.

Over the fifty-six years that Amy spent in India, she faced many challenges and terrifying experiences. Though she had legitimate reasons to be afraid, she felt God leading her beyond her fears to trust in the Lord. In all her interactions, God led her on a journey from fear to friendship.

Amy's friendship with the Lord sustained her. Her friendships with her Indian sisters in Christ encouraged her to carry on. And her relationships with beautiful Indian people, who were not yet believers, inspired her to keep praying for the day when they, too, might encounter the transforming love of Christ.

She found that writing was a form of enlisting broader prayer support for the work in India. She wrote *Things as They Are* (1905) and *Overweights of Joy* (1906) as a way of sharing with family and friends in Europe about the grim difficulties she and her band were facing on the field. Over her long sojourn in India, she wrote more than thirty books that impacted readers around the world.[20]

At the beginning of *Overweights of Joy*, she observes: "If this book's atmosphere is dark it is because the gods, the giant powers which lie behind the subtle systems of our day, still exist in strength and force. The song is sung in the night: let no one dream the night has passed."[21]

Lord, give us courage to join in the song that is sung in the night and to keep hoping for the time when the night will pass. Lord, help us to choose friendship with You and to trust you to sustain us as we try to live lives of loving service in this broken world.

Seeing Fears Transformed by Friendships

But, when all is said, there is still this to remember, we need not fear to be too small. The greatest Book in the world (like life itself) has many pages of small things.

—Amy Carmichael, *Tables in the Wilderness*[22]

---

19 Carmichael, *Beginning of a Story*, Kindle ed., 746.

20 Kommers states that Amy wrote some 36 books, although some of these were only written for the Dohnavur family and not sold internationally. *Triumphant Love*, Kindle ed., 254.

21 Carmichael, *Overweights of Joy*, Kindle ed., 532.

22 Carmichael, *Tables in the Wilderness*, Kindle ed., 9103.

From the window next to my top bunk, I looked into the back alleyway and watched rats scurrying around a dumpster. A few figures walked past, calling out for their next "fix." This was my first night in the "Downtown Eastside" neighborhood of Vancouver, British Columbia, where I would be living for the next few months in preparation for moving into a slum with "Servants,"[23] an international network of Jesus-following, justice-loving people who serve among urban poor communities throughout Asia. For a long time, I lay awake, listening to the night sounds of my new home, wondering if this neighborhood ever slept.

Months of prayer, preparation, and anticipation had led to the moment when my bus pulled into Vancouver's Union Station at 1 a.m. that July morning in 2010. I had said goodbye to my beloved friends, family, and church community, thinking that I would not see them again for another three years. I had traveled by Amtrak train from the East Coast to the West Coast of the United States, then taken a bus across the border into Canada. From my bus window in Union Station, I saw two young women wearing patched jeans and hoodies, whom I guessed were waiting to pick me up. As I stepped off the bus with my guitar and duffle bag, they greeted me with hugs.

Lying in my bunk listening to the rats in the dumpster below my window that first night, I retraced our late-night walk from Union Station to this Servants' team house on Hastings Street, each block crowded with people— drug dealers stationed on every corner shouting the names of narcotics, men and women of all ages twitching and muttering as they waited for their fix, shapeless bodies sprawled along the sidewalks, hunched figures scraping the ground, searching for discarded cigarette butts. Exhausted from my travels, my mind continued to swirl from all that I had seen and heard on that short walk, but eventually I drifted off to sleep, and a few short hours later, the first light of the midsummer Vancouver sun finally roused me to greet my new home by daylight.

The following days were filled with getting to know my team—three couples (each with two young children), two single women, and two single guys. I was considered a "preparer," as I was joining the team for a short time before heading to a slum community in Asia. We shared team rhythms, such as morning and evening prayer, formation nights, business meetings, and dinners. The dinners were a community affair, open to anyone in the Downtown Eastside. We took turns cooking, which was a learning curve in creativity and spontaneity, as most of our groceries came from donated boxes of food, and whoever was cooking had a mere twenty-dollar budget beyond whatever we could find in the fridge to feed from twenty to forty people.

---

23 Servants to Asia's Urban Poor. See www.servantsasia.org.

During the weeks that followed, I spent my days learning about the Downtown Eastside while also praying about where I might land in Asia. The Downtown Eastside is a unique place and one of the oldest neighborhoods in Vancouver, but it is also home to a variety of complex social issues: homelessness, drug use, poverty, crime, mental illness, and the sex trade. Because of these issues, the neighborhood is also filled with numerous Christian and non-Christian groups who are trying to "make a difference," and so soup kitchens, homeless shelters, and drop-in centers can be found on almost every block.

Gentrification has also transformed the edges of the Downtown Eastside into places of tourism and wealth. Just a stone's throw away from drug dealers, I would see double-decker tourist buses pass by on their drive around the beautiful city. Many days, I walked ten minutes from our Servants house to Crab Park, a sandy beach where I would swim, enjoy a view of the ocean, and sit or pray in solitude. From the beach, I could see Carnival Cruise ships docked just a few blocks away. Other days, I followed the gorgeous six-mile (10 km) bike and walking path around the Stanley Park Seawall. I found it difficult to reconcile the incredible beauty all around Vancouver with the brokenness and pain of the Downtown Eastside.

> *I spent my days learning about the Downtown Eastside while also praying about where I might land in Asia.*

As I befriended women in my neighborhood, I met many uniquely beautiful people. Katie had memorized all the area codes in North America and would ask people where they were from and then rattle off their area code. Abi, a First Nations woman, was in the middle of a court case trying to regain custody rights for her eleven-year-old daughter, who had run away. Susie showed me where to find wild berries at Crab Park. These and countless other women in the Downtown Eastside had experienced trauma, abuse, addiction, and pain, and yet they regularly amazed me with their kindness and generosity.

My time in the Downtown Eastside stirred me to think about what Jesus meant when he said, "Blessed are you who are poor, for yours is the kingdom of God" (Luke 6:20). The people in the Downtown Eastside have access to pretty much every basic human need (except, perhaps, dignity)—free food, showers, laundry, places to sleep. And yet I think that these are some of the people that Jesus was talking about when he said, "Blessed are the poor."

Once a week, the women on our team would engage in a time of "Night Vision," walking the streets, looking for opportunities to initiate conversations with women involved in the sex industry and invite them back to our community garden or team office for snacks and conversation. As we listened to stories from these neighborhood women, I was confronted with my sheltered and privileged upbringing and realized that I was like "the rich young ruler" in Mark's gospel (10:17–27) and needed help walking away from the wealth that "so easily entangles" (Heb 12:1 NIV).[24]

Yet I also realized that the desires of wealth can also entangle the poor. Beth, a First Nations woman whose mother was an alcoholic, was taken away from her mother when she was only eighteen months old and put into a foster family. Her foster parents had five children of their own, along with Beth and another First Nations foster girl. She told me her story with a blank face, as if talking about someone else: "The foster dad sexually abused me and the other First Nations foster girl while we were growing up. But I never told anyone because I loved my foster mom and did not want to hurt her. They were an 'upstanding family.'"

As a young teenager, Beth kept running away, looking for her birth mom. She only knew the name of her hometown and her mom's first name— Dorine. She went around asking people, "Are you my mother?" trying to find anyone by the name of Dorine. Eventually, Beth did find her mom, but the reunion was mixed, as Beth had been carrying so much anger towards her mom for so many years.

Eventually, Beth got married, but it was a dysfunctional relationship, and her husband was abusive. One night, she tried to take her children and escape, but her husband came after them with a shotgun. "You can leave," he said, "but you aren't taking my kids." She left and ended up staying with a friend in Vancouver, who was addicted to crack cocaine and paid for her addiction by being a "working girl." Before long, Beth became addicted as well and started working as a prostitute to pay for the drugs.

I heard many similar stories.

Yet each victim of abuse and trauma is a real person with a name, favorite color, and some kind of family. As I heard story after story of pain and brokenness, I struggled to maintain hope, wondering what it meant to proclaim Christ's "good news" in a place like the Downtown Eastside.[25]

---

24 While the verse from Hebrews is "sin that so easily entangles," I am reminded of the story that Jesus tells about the four types of soil. "As for what fell among the thorns, these are the ones who hear; but as they go on their way, they are choked by the cares and riches and pleasures of life, and their fruit does not mature" (Luke 8:14). I literally picture the wealth entangling the growing shoots, choking them from bearing fruit.

25 I wrote the poem "Freedom Rains" as I reflected on Beth's story. You can find the poem in the appendix of Anita Rahma, *Beyond Our Walls*.

A few weeks after I arrived in Vancouver, I accompanied Beth to a local drop-in center for women involved in the sex industry. Strategically hidden in a back alley, it has no sign and is protected by barbed wire, high fences, and a security guard. There are more than four hundred members, who are either currently working or have worked in the sex industry at some point. I was not supposed to be allowed to enter, but Beth brought me in, and no one seemed to notice. We walked through a room with a large plasma screen TV, a shower and make-up room, a clothes room, a computer room, and a room with a phone. As I looked around at all the women inside who worked as prostitutes at night, I wondered what Jesus's love might mean to them—and what I, a sheltered twenty-two-year-old college graduate, could possibly offer in this context.

> As I heard story after story of pain and brokenness, I struggled to maintain hope, wondering what it meant to proclaim Christ's "good news" in a place like the Downtown Eastside.

While engaging in life in the Downtown Eastside, I also continued to sense a deep call to Asia. I began visiting an Indonesian church, praying about joining the Jakarta team. When my parents and brothers came to visit me over American Thanksgiving, we all went to this church together. As none of us spoke Indonesian, the congregation graciously provided us with headsets so we could listen to simultaneous translation.

I do not remember the Scripture passage the preacher was speaking on, but I do remember that he gave an illustration about someone ministering in a slum community in Africa. My interest piqued, as I was praying about moving into an urban poor community in Jakarta. The pastor shared how hundreds from this slum community had met Jesus, and then he said something I have never forgotten, "And one by one they all became millionaires, just like the disciples."

If I had only heard this myself, I probably would have thought I *misheard* it, but my whole family was wearing the translation headsets, and we all looked at each other and stifled uncomfortable laughs. After the service, we wondered if the translator had mis-translated what the preacher had said or if he was preaching a prosperity gospel theology from the pulpit: "And one by one they all became millionaires, just like the disciples."

Of course, the disciples did *not* become millionaires! They became servants of the gospel, which ultimately led all of them to be killed—except for John, who was exiled for the rest of his life to a remote island. While we may want to believe that following Jesus leads to comfort, safety, and wealth, the Bible shares a very different story.

Though most Christians might not *say* they believe that following Jesus will lead to economic success, many of us might *live* as if we believe it. We may believe that if we go to church, help with Sunday school, and have our daily quiet time, things should go well with us. And we in the West often live as if we believe that we are entitled to prosperity because we've earned it, and we think we are being blessed by God because of our orthodox beliefs. But Jesus calls us to lay down our dreams of economic success and seek his kingdom, and as followers of Christ, worldly riches can no longer be our aim.

Living among the poor in the Downtown Eastside while attending middle-class church on Sunday mornings raised many questions within me that did not have easy answers. I have continued to ask similar questions since moving into a slum in Jakarta. As I learn to trust Jesus as my savior and king each day, he continues to lead me into unlikely places of pain, brokenness, and seeming danger. My challenge is to *believe* that I can meet Jesus in all these places and to trust that he is with me—and also with those around me—even in the darkest valleys.

Jesus, help us to see you in the hidden places.
May you guide us beyond our fears into deeper friendship with you,
enabling us to love those around us.

Encountering Jesus in Places of Addiction

Surely any loss were well while that we may know Him, and the power of His resurrection, and the fellowship of His sufferings, that from the darker gift of pain, may come forth the brighter gift of service. A fuller passing on of those unsearchable riches than could have been possible, had He not called us to follow Him through the very shadow of death, where He keeps His treasures of darkness.

—Amy Carmichael, *From Sunrise Land: Letters from Japan*[26]

"Sally, are you okay?" my Servants teammate called out to a figure who was hunched on the sidewalk of a street corner, clearly having a bad "trip." Whatever cocktail of drugs she had taken was causing her a lot of pain, and she was shaking uncontrollably—a tragic and frequent sight in Vancouver's Downtown Eastside. A woman standing nearby told us that Sally had been like this for two hours. Though we were on our way to worship in a nearby park, we quickly changed our plans and plopped down next to Sally.

---

26 Carmichael, *From Sunrise Land*, Kindle ed., 41.

For the next hour or two, we held her, prayed for her, cried with her, and sang over her as hundreds of people walked by and dealers sold drugs all around us. Eventually, an ambulance came, but it could not take Sally without her consent, which she refused to give. Though the Vancouver fall air was cold, Sally kept pulling off her blanket as she thrashed about, grinding her teeth. She kicked her shoes off, then clutched my hand as if hanging on for her life, begging me to pull her out of her torment.

As we prayed for Sally and held her skeleton of a body, I became acutely aware of God's presence with us. I sensed Jesus, the Good Shepherd, desperately longing to gather Sally, his lost sheep, into his arms. This image of Christ grieving for Sally and longing to hold her moved me deeply.

Broken by years of addiction, poverty, and abuse, Sally was in a physical hell as she wept and gnashed her teeth on that street corner, her emaciated body convulsing wildly. Yet in the midst of her physical suffering, she was surprisingly present, answering our questions and joining us when we sang "Amazing Grace." When we asked her how she would like us to pray, she said, "For my parents: Mama and Ray." As we prayed, she clutched the blue plastic rosary that was hanging around her neck.

As she started to "come down" from her trip, she kept saying, "I'm starving." She had a bag of crackers that had been crushed by her clenched fists, but as her body grew calm, she was able to reach her shaking hand into the plastic bag and thrust the crumbs into her mouth. "I don't want to eat alone," she said, insisting that we share some of the crumbs. Once she was stable, we went to get some food from our house. After taking a bite of a strawberry, Sally offered some to me. Her desire to share reminded me of communion: crackers, broken and crushed into pieces as Christ's broken body, a red strawberry as Christ's blood. I sensed that the sidewalk where we were sitting together, sharing this feast, was holy ground.

During my time in the Downtown Eastside, I came to know many starving women. In their hungry eyes, sunken cheeks, tight faces, jutting collarbones, wispy hair, and junior-sized baggy jeans covering stick-thin, wobbly legs, I saw a reflection of those suffering from an anorexic eating disorder.

In these painfully thin women, I saw myself. When I was fourteen and just beginning high school, I moved with my family to the Philippines and became convinced that I was fat. I don't know if this delusion was triggered by the stress of moving to a new culture,[27] or because I was surrounded by so many undernourished people, or by the millions of media images of unrealistic, unhealthy female bodies that I had seen over my lifetime—a constant

---

27 My family spent three years in the Philippines when I was in high school.

bombardment from my American culture to the rest of the world. But by the end of my first year of high school, I had decided that I had to lose weight.

What started as a perfectionistic pursuit of "health"—eating fruit and a small serving of carbs for breakfast, cutting out butter and jam—quickly slipped into anorexia. This eating disorder is a lie that infiltrates young minds under the guise of beauty, health, and youth. She is a demon that consumes all your thoughts, controls you with fear, casts you under her spell, and convinces you that *you have everything in control. She may begin as your friend and only confidante, but she will slowly destroy you.*

One lie of eating disorders is that the whole world revolves around *you*—as if everyone notices if you weigh five pounds more (or less) than you did last week, or if your stomach is a little bigger (or smaller) than it was two months ago, or if you eat a cookie or piece of candy (or nothing at all). Anorexia paralyzed me in a prison of seductively self-consuming thoughts, for there was no room for me to care for others, because I could not think of anything beyond what I was going to make for my next mini-meal. This experience became a sort of living death, where I was unable to think about anything but food and my weight, unable to enjoy a birthday cake or a day without exercise, unable to eat three meals a day.

Anorexia is also an easily hidden and often socially acceptable disease in our culture—until young people start passing out or need to be hospitalized. In fact, those silently struggling with eating disorders are often held up as beautiful, for many are models and stars, while others are our classmates, roommates, or family members. One in ten people who are diagnosed with anorexia eventually die. Countless others die when their hearts stop beating, but their deaths are never linked to an eating disorder. Though our bodies are amazingly resilient, they are also fragile. If we refuse to feed our bodies, we will eventually shut down.

After a year of descending down this dangerous path of lies—such as believing that carrots were fattening!—the Lord intervened in my life through the truth-speaking of my parents, a supportive group of friends, and an encounter with the Holy Spirit. Suddenly, the scales that had been shielding me from the truth came off my eyes, and I could finally see the skeleton that I had become. I felt a bit like Paul must have felt after Ananias prayed for him and his sight was restored, for as I encountered the truth, I became suddenly aware of the awful lies I had been living and began to weep.

While I believed that Christ was more powerful than my eating disorder, my recovery had many painful relapses and setbacks. Over the course of my long journey of healing, I have had to relearn how to eat, and I have also had to ingest truths that will combat the lies that the destructive power of anorexia wants me to believe. Following are some of the key truths that have nourished me along the way. First, *I am fearfully and wonderfully made* (Ps 139:14). Second, the Lord loves me even if I am not perfect, *for his power is perfected in my weakness* (2 Cor 12:9). Third, no matter what the number on the scale might say, the Lord loves me as I am, for *there is no fear in love, and his perfect love will cast out my fear* (1 John 4:18), so *I do not need to be afraid* (Jer 42:11).

So many girls are struggling with the evil shackles of eating disorders, but they are often isolated in the prison of their own agony. Though many are engaged in the same battle, fighting against a common enemy, we are too afraid to talk about it because we believe the lie that we are all alone.

> *So many girls are ... isolated in the prison of their own agony.*

The silence around this lie is maddening for me, and yet my own silence often seems easier than sharing my own personal journey. But if we are following Jesus as our way, truth, and life, we must teach our sisters and daughters, brothers and sons that the images we see in "beauty" magazines, billboards, movies, television, and all over the internet are false. We must speak out the life-giving truth of God's love for each of us and denounce the lies that have come to steal our self-worth and destroy us (John 10:10).

Together, our communities must remember the beauty of eating by celebrating the baking of bread, growing nourishing food in our gardens, cooking delicious food, savoring the tastes of each meal, seeking to share an abundant life together, and welcoming all to our tables. Rather than chasing the addictive idol of a perfect or ideal body, we must help one another behold the beauty in each and every one of our bodies, and we must receive our bodies as precious gifts that God has given us to tend and keep in the same way that we are called to care for the earth that sustains us (Gen 2:15).

In the Downtown Eastside of Vancouver, which is known as the "most livable city" in North America, I encountered hundreds of people struggling with addictions to drugs and alcohol, and in these neighbors and friends (like Sally), I saw a reflection of my own addiction. Yet the women of the Downtown Eastside, who literally prostitute themselves to feed their addictions, do not have the means to hide behind nice clothes, hairstyles, or makeup. They do not have an education to shield themselves with an illusion of health and wellbeing. Rather, their thinness is a direct result of drug abuse—of forgetting to eat and walking miles and miles collecting bottles to get money for their next fix—or AIDS or some other disease.

Addictions are everywhere, but Jesus has words of love, truth, and healing to speak to the millions of girls and boys in America who desperately need to be freed from the bondage of anorexia and bulimia—and to my friends in the Downtown Eastside, who desperately need to be freed from their addictions, too.

Lord, free us from ourselves. Help us to surrender to your love. Help us to move from fear of the scales to being friends with our own bodies. Help us to move beyond our addictions into the freedom that you offer.

Room to Reflect

What particular moments stand out to you from Amy's story?

As you reflect on your own life, what fears do you sense Jesus inviting you to recognize?

How might God be inviting you to relinquish those fears?

Read John 15:12–15.
Spend some time dwelling on the truth that God loves you and desires friendship with you.

Invitation 2

From Self to Surrender

God give us a pure passion of love that knows nothing of hesitation and grudging, and measuring, nothing of compromise! What if it seem impossible to face all that surrender may mean? Is there not provision for the impossible?

—Amy Carmichael, *Lotus Buds*[1]

You are God and I am not

When I am weak, you carry me safe through the storm,
safe through the storm.

You are God and I am not, when I fall down,
You lift me up once again, up once again.

Oh God, oh God. I'm surrounded by grace.

Oh Lord, oh Lord. You give us your strength.

Help me to trust you're good, Trust your love,
Trust your plans for me.

Help me to trust your grace, Trust your hope,
Trust you are God and I'm not

—From "You Are God and I Am Not"[2]

Every day we are bombarded with the lie that the world revolves around us (or should revolve around us). With the use of smartphones, a constant stream of advertising lulls us into believing that we are the center of the universe. But throughout history, followers of Christ have been invited to choose a different path of surrendering our wills to God. Jesus left his followers with the powerful prayer that echoes across time and cultures: "Not my will, but yours be done."[3]

---

1 Carmichael, *Lotus Buds*, Kindle ed., 989.
2 This is an excerpt from a song I wrote in 2013.
3 Luke 22:42.

When we decide to follow Jesus, we are invited to surrender our whole self to God, which continues to be a choice we must make every day. Will we choose to put our will first or the will of God? Will we seek our own good or the good of those around us? Will we follow our savior, Jesus, by sacrificially offering our time, energy, and life to those around us—or will we listen to the world that teaches us to hoard everything and to serve ourselves?

The voices of the world shout out to us, promising us happiness if we purchase the latest gadget, a larger house, or go on a dream vacation. But if we chase all these offers, we will end up with full hands but empty hearts. Amy invites her readers to root themselves in the only One who offers real peace. A life of downward discipleship is, by definition, a life of surrender. As we surrender ourselves to the Lord and trust him to provide for us, we will be led into a more intimate friendship with him and a deeper faith that he will always be with us.

> *A life of downward discipleship is, by definition, a life of surrender.*

Asking Amy: *How can we find peace?*

What of the girl by the fireside crushing down the sense of an Under-call that will not let her rest? The work to which that Call would lead her will not be anything great: it will only mean little humble everyday doings wherever she is sent. But if the Call is a true Call from heaven, it will change to a song as she obeys; and through all the afterward of life, through all the loneliness that may come, through all the disillusions… then and for ever that song of the Lord will sing itself through the quiet places of her soul, and she will be sure—with the sureness that is just pure peace—that she is where her Master meant her to be.

—Amy Carmichael, *Lotus Buds*[4]

One day when Amy was still a teenager in Belfast, she was on her way home with some of her siblings after a church service. As they were walking, they noticed an old lady coming down the street, heavily laden down with bundles. It was clear this old woman was poor, as she was dressed in rags.

At that moment, Amy and her brothers decided to help the old woman even though it felt very uncomfortable for them to do so.[5] For in order to relieve the woman of her bundles and accompany her along her way, they first had to turn around and face all the "respectably dressed" people who

---

4 Carmichael, *Lotus Buds*, Kindle ed., 991.
5 Amy tells this story in her book *Gold Cord*, 2–3.

were walking home from church. This moment was a turning point in Amy's life that became engraved in her memory as she heard an audible voice say, "gold, silver, precious stones, wood, hay, stubble; every man's work shall be made manifest: for the day shall declare it, because it shall be revealed by fire; and the fire shall try every man's work of what sort it is" (1 Cor 3:12–13 KJV).

From this point on, Amy knew that she must spend her life on things that mattered for eternity. She knew this call would mean surrendering herself to follow Jesus, even if that led to ridicule and suffering.[6] Once Amy moved to India, she continued to remember this moment as a teenager, a lesson of obedience to the nudging of the Spirit—even at the risk of receiving contempt from those around her.

For as Dohnavur Fellowship's work rescuing girls from the Hindu temple system continued to grow, Amy and her team faced misunderstandings and scorn from many sides. Even other European missionaries disagreed with Amy's work, as they felt that things could not be as bad for these girls as Amy said they were. Under British rule,[7] they did not think temple prostitution still existed.[8] Why make such a stir? Many missionaries also disagreed with Amy's decision to wear Indian clothes and work so closely with Indian teammates. Many letters that Amy received in response to her books were full of questions and rebukes: why try to convert Hindus to Christianity anyway? why take the gospel somewhere that it is not wanted? why not leave change to the government?

But Amy believed that she was listening to her Master's voice, and this is all that mattered to her. Though these other voices were sounding loudly all around her, she was marching to the beat of a different drummer.[9]

As she and her band of missionaries gave themselves to raising the children they rescued, they were taking part in a crash-course of trusting God to provide for their needs in his timing, as they did not have bank accounts overflowing with money. With a growing family to feed, educate, and support, this required them to surrender to God and trust him for everything.

---

6 For more information, watch Oliver and Greene, "Story of Amy Carmichael and the Dohnavur Fellowship (2005)."

7 At this time, India was not yet independent from England.

8 In fact, it was not until 1934 that the first law was passed to begin to improve the rights of the *Devadasi* women (Bombay Devadasi Protection Act, see Kommers, *Triumphant Love*, Kindle ed., 372). With India's independence in 1947, further legislation was passed to prohibit the traffic of children for temple purposes. And then a nationwide prohibition was passed in 1954. However, the practice continued illegally for many years. Furthermore, the traffic of children for prostitution still is a huge problem throughout India and the world today. See Kommers, *Triumphant Love*, Kindle ed., 381.

9 This now-familiar analogy comes from Henry David Thoreau's *Walden*, where he writes: "If a man does not keep pace with his companions, perhaps it is because he hears a different drummer. Let him step to the music which he hears, however measured or far away."

In the books that Amy wrote, she shares both beautiful stories about the amazing work of the Lord as well as countless stories of intense suffering. The Dohnavur family lost many children and coworkers to sickness and disease. At the beginning, they were days away from the nearest hospital, and it was often difficult to acquire the necessary medicines when illnesses spread. Amy asked many difficult questions in her writings: how could the Lord bring children to them, only to have the children die in their arms? why were children who had been rescued from such pain and trauma, who were finally finding healing and joy at Dohnavur, snatched away by sickness?

Taking care of hundreds of children was not the missionary work that Amy imagined when she moved to India as an itinerate preacher. But she and her "Starry Cluster"[10] missionary band were "allowing their feet to be tied" for the love of the children, an Indian saying about motherhood that Amy adopted for her band. Their commitment to root themselves at Dohnavur in order to love and care for the children entrusted to them was also a call to "allow their feet to be tied" to the cross of Christ and to carry that cross wherever he might lead them.

In 1931, when Amy was in her sixties, she had an accident as she was visiting a building site. It was getting dark, and she fell into a hole that she could not see and broke her leg, dislocated an ankle, and injured her spine. This accident left her in pain for the rest of her life, barely able to get out of bed. From her sickbed at Dohnavur, she penned many of her most profound books about suffering.[11]

Her years of service in India, along with her years in bed unable to walk, taught Amy how to keep choosing to die to herself and surrender to God's will—and then to accept it.

In Amy's journey with God, she discovered that peace cannot be found by forgetting the world's pain, nor by endeavoring to solve everything—neither in aloofness nor even in submission. Rather, as she writes in her poem, "In Acceptance Lieth Peace":

> He said, "I will accept the breaking sorrow
> Which God to-morrow
> Will to His son explain."

---

10 "Starry Cluster" was the name used by Indian neighbors to refer to the band of missionary women during their early years of ministry (discussed in *Lotus Buds*). In later years, Amy often referred to their group as the "Dohnavur Fellowship" (abbreviated as DF) or simply "the Family."

11 *Rose From Brier* (1933), *Gold by Moonlight* (1935), *Toward Jerusalem* (1936), *Figures of the True* (1938), *If* (1938), and *Kohila* (1939) are some of the beautiful books she penned during this time.

Then did the turmoil deep within him cease.
Not vain the word, not vain:
For in Acceptance lieth peace.[12]

Such acceptance does not mean *giving up the fight to make the world a better place.* As we can see from Amy's life, she did not just *accept* the injustices around her; however, over many years of journeying with the Lord, Amy learned that oftentimes God's answer is, "no." She learned that God does not always appear to deliver our hopes and desires—at least not on our timetable. She learned that the Lord's ways are mysterious—and that the Lord both gives and takes away. Yet she continued to sing with the prophet Job, "The LORD gave, and the LORD has taken away: blessed be the name of the LORD" (Job 1:21).

> *Amy learned that oftentimes God's answer is, "no."*

Amy believed that she was tending work that was much bigger than herself. She knew that the story God was writing with her life was not about her, but Jesus. Even when babies were sick, coworkers tragically died, court cases were brought against her, and people around her screamed, "Jesus is nothing compared to Hinduism," she trusted that God was at work. She accepted both the good and the hard, the beautiful and the tragic, the "yesses" and the "noes" from her Lord. Even if she could not understand all these things, she accepted them.

Help us surrender our lives to you, Lord. Free us to choose to follow where you are leading, even when it leads us to disgrace and pain. Help us to accept that your ways are not our ways and that we can only see a small part of your larger story. Help us trust that you are weaving something beautiful, even if what we see looks like a tangled mess.

Surrendering to God's Timing

But singing hymns from a distance will never save souls. By God's grace, coming and giving and praying will. Are we prepared for this? Or would we rather sing? Searcher of hearts, turn Thy search-light upon us! Are we coming, giving, praying till it hurts? Are we praying, yea agonising in prayer? or is prayer but "a pleasant exercise"—a holy relief for our feelings?

—Amy Carmichael, *Things as They Are*[13]

---

12 Carmichael, *Made in the Pans*, Kindle ed., 1520.
13 Carmichael, *Things as They Are*, Kindle ed., 497.

After spending almost half a year in Vancouver, I joined the Servants team serving in Jakarta, Indonesia in 2011. The lessons that I had learned in Canada about moving past fear and towards friendship continued in the context of this Asian mega-city, where Jesus was inviting me to follow him into a slum community.

Getting on an airplane and landing halfway around the world did not make me a different person. I was my same self, but now surrounded by a Muslim community, a foreign language, and a completely different culture. Every day, I was challenged to surrender my sense of control over what might happen, to surrender to God's Spirit at work, and to surrender my sense of identity by allowing God to mold me and shape me in this new context.

> There were other things about myself that I had to completely leave behind.

Living in a slum community, I experienced evictions, floods, fires, and diseases along with my neighbors.[14] On any given day, I did not know who might come knocking at my door or what crisis or dilemma might face me. I had to surrender ideas about what it means to be "on time" and my understanding of doing something in a "timely" manner.

When I was in high school, while our family was living in the Philippines, we ordered a new washing machine from a nearby mall, and they agreed to deliver it within a few hours. We went home and waited and waited. Finally, my mom called the store and asked what time we should expect it. "Before five, or after five," the friendly Filipino told my mom on the phone. Finally, they delivered the washer at around seven. Expectations about time are very different in different cultures.

In the States, I often thought I knew the "right" way of doing something, but in Jakarta, there were so many things that I did *not* know how to do and the way my neighbors did things was *different* than I wanted it to be. In small things—how I peeled carrots, how I hung up laundry, how I placed my spoon on a plate after finishing eating—my neighbors gave me new instructions. I needed to humble myself and surrender to the process of learning, though sometimes it felt humiliating.

There were other things about myself that I had to completely leave behind. In high school and college, I played tennis every day for multiple hours. It was time-consuming and fun, but I realized that tennis was something I needed to surrender. I could not expect to play tennis while living in a slum community. And while writing these words now, many years

---

14 To read more of these stories, see Rahma, *Beyond Our Walls*.

after the fact, I no longer feel emotionally attached to tennis. But at the time, it seemed like a large sacrifice the Lord was asking me to make.

I realized that there are many things to which Westerners feel entitled. We talk a lot about "rights" and "entitlements," but I was learning that Jesus talks about *surrender*. He invites us to pick up our cross and follow him—and this is not an invitation to a beautiful, decorative cross, but an instrument of torture and death. Jesus calls his followers on this journey because that is the upside-down way of Jesus—surrendering rights and privileges for the sake of seeking the kingdom of God, for in surrender, we find freedom.

Before moving to a slum, I felt entitled to private space, alone time, a carefully crafted schedule about what I would accomplish each day, and access to exercise whenever I wanted. Living in Jakarta, I was invited to surrender these negotiable things so that I could learn new ways of being. Though I needed to incorporate rhythms of self-care so that my life in the slum would be sustainable over a longer term, I also needed to sacrifice some of those *privileges* so that Christ could teach me to trust him for what I really *needed*.

One of the hardest things for me to surrender were my hopes around our Servants team. I desperately hoped for teammates who would serve alongside me for the long term, but over the years, teammates kept coming and going. Different gifts, passions, challenges, and needs brought people to our team for a time—and then caused them to leave. This constant parade of people in and out of our team life exhausted me and my husband.

> Rural poverty and urban poverty are different.

How could we continue to trust and open ourselves to new teammates? How could we continue to invest in relationships with teammates, knowing that the relationships might only last a few months or a few years?

But in my journey with our team over the past thirteen years, the Lord has been teaching me to surrender to the process of a growing, fluctuating, changing community—and to trust the Lord. I am learning to appreciate each person who comes and journeys alongside our neighbors in the slums of Jakarta.

For a variety of reasons, for over six years now, we have not had any teammates from outside of Indonesia. Our interns and teammates who come from different Bible schools in Indonesia also have much to learn. For many of them, living simply is not difficult, as they have grown up in families struggling with poverty. But rural poverty and urban poverty are different, and so they must adjust to the constant noise, smells of trash, and close proximity of having people around all the time. And they also have to adjust to living in a Muslim community.

Although Indonesia has the largest Muslim population of any country in the world, Bible school students tend to come from communities that were almost exclusively Christian. We are privileged to guide them on a journey of breaking down stereotypes and prejudices, and it is beautiful to watch them learn to love and receive love from our neighbors. This journey is not only for the interns, but also for their families and church communities back home, for as they share stories of what they are learning in this Islamic neighborhood, enemies become humanized, and fears are transformed into friendships.

In a Muslim context, our team is continually challenged to rethink how we communicate the gospel. Can we do so in respectful ways? Can we surrender our Westernized concept of Christianity as we seek to be understood by our Muslim friends? Even though we are "free" to eat pork, drink alcohol, wear different clothes, and blast "Christian" music, we are invited to lay these "rights" down at the foot of the cross so that we do not create stumbling blocks for our Muslim friends. We do not want them to reject the gospel and Jesus because they are rejecting Western culture. Instead, through our loving and respectful presence in the neighborhood, we hope they will encounter Jesus, *Isa Al-Masih*, who loves them and cares for them.

I am sure we are not doing anything perfectly, but together, our team is learning to die to ourselves and to pick up our crosses and follow Jesus in this place.

Lord, help us as we seek to surrender to you each day. May our hearts be formed to beat in sync with yours as we love, care, and give sacrificially to the people around us. Teach us what it means to say "yes" to you over and over and over again.

Surrendering to a Lifetime of Learning

Praying alone is not enough, but oh for more real praying! We are playing at praying, and caring, and coming; playing at doing—if doing costs—playing at everything but play. We are earnest enough about that. God open our eyes and convict us of our insincerity! Burn out the superficial in us, make us intensely in earnest! And may God quicken our sympathy, and touch our heart, and nerve our arm for what will prove a desperate fight.

—Amy Carmichael, *Things as They Are*[15]

When I first moved to Indonesia, a friend told me, "Foreigners are like elephants. Even if their intentions are good, they end up hurting people in the process." How could I avoid this all-too-common pitfall of foreigners creating harm in the process of trying to do good?

In my journey, I have realized how important it is for us to choose to come into a new context as a *learner*. This will involve inviting our neighbors to be our teachers and humbling ourselves to receive help from those around us as we seek to learn the culture, language, and way of life in our new home.

In April or May of 2014, after I had been living in Jakarta for a few years, there was a big rainstorm in our neighborhood. The wind blew so strongly that two of our asbestos roof tiles flew off our house. While asbestos is considered a very dangerous material in the West, it is a common roofing material in many countries. The tiles are about the same size as a piece of corrugated metal, but they are insulated and so do not heat up as much as metal roofing. Without the tiles, rain began to pour into our house.

As I stood in our bedroom, holding our baby son, I watched the water and wondered what to do.

Suddenly, I heard a voice and thumping behind our house. I looked out the window, and as the rain came down in sheets—lightning flashing and thunder roaring—I saw a neighbor climbing a ladder carrying a blue tarp, which he spread over the gaping hole of our roof. I was humbled and amazed at his care for our family, his willingness to sacrifice his own comfort and safety to help us.

I watched him climb down the ladder and then wave goodbye, and I felt a wave of gratitude for his practical help and lovingkindness. Hugging my baby son, I breathed a prayer of relief and thanksgiving that water was no longer pouring into our home.

---

15 Carmichael, *Things as They Are*, Kindle ed., 466.

As a foreigner in Indonesia, I have learned so much from my Indonesian friends about service, community, and caring for those around me. In my journey, I have had to learn that I am not a savior, but I am coming alongside beautiful people who are capable of doing beautiful things.

About two years after moving to Jakarta, our team opened "House of Hope," a small learning center, where we taught kindergarten students and ran an afterschool program for children. After about six years of importing Christian teachers (a mixture of foreigner and Indonesian teammates), we realized that we could invite women from the neighborhood to teach *with* us. Even though most had not finished middle school, we felt that we could train and equip them as teachers. We watched with joy and awe as they gained self-confidence and became fabulous teachers, loving and serving children from their very own neighborhood! This experience was a gift for the kids—and a gift for us!

> I have learned so much from my Indonesian friends about service, community, and caring for those around me.

In attempting missionary work, we can become religious elephants, stomping around, making a scene, and often crushing whatever new sprouts might be growing. We have seen churches drive into our community in fancy cars, open the trunk, and wait for the crowd of people to rush to get whatever is free. One time, a church group came in and invited our neighbors to a birthday party. The "birthday party" turned out to be a Christmas service at a church, and the parents who went along with their children were very angry afterward.

In our Muslim context, such mission outreaches grieve me, as they leave a negative impression on our Muslim neighbors, who may then perceive Christians as wealthy people who put on a show, give out free stuff, and are often deceptive. Such "hit and run" missions often do not help our neighbors encounter the love of Jesus or learn about his upside-down kingdom, and unfortunately, they have a lasting impact on how Muslims view Christ and his followers.

Though Jesus used all sorts of illustrations to describe the kingdom of God, he never referred to anything large, strong, and powerful (such as an elephant!). Instead, Jesus chose humble, seemingly insignificant things to describe the kingdom of God—yeast, a mustard seed, a hidden treasure—that start out small, but can grow into something with a surprisingly large impact.

When I was living in Vancouver, I remember being on a prayer retreat and reading through the Gospels. As I sat on a grassy field, praying and listening, I felt like the Lord was giving me a new metaphor for the kingdom of God: *spiderwebs.* At first, I wondered why God would give me such an image? Why would the kingdom be like spiderwebs?

As I was looked out across the field at all the lovely green blades of grass, a sunbeam suddenly revealed the glistening beauty of dew caught on all the spiderwebs covering the field. And while I looked at the intricate threads of sparkling silk, it occurred to me how spiders spin their webs in all sorts of places—under beds, in the corners of ceilings, and also in the palaces of kings and queens! I realized that the kingdom of God is like spiderwebs—present in all sorts of places, sometimes invisible and yet suddenly, in the right light, surprisingly visible.

A decade after this retreat, I was reading a book about animal trivia to my two boys before bed. Imagine my surprise when I read that spider silk is actually considered one of the strongest materials on earth. Although we can "break" a single spiderweb, if the spider silk is woven together, it becomes extremely strong—some sources even claim it is stronger than steel!

Jesus, help us surrender our preconceived ideas about your kingdom so that we will tread softly as we move into new cultures. Forgive our foreigner elephant blunders and shine your dazzling light so that we can see the people and places around us as you see them.

Room to Reflect

What new details stand out to you from Amy's story?

As you reflect on your own life, how do you sense God inviting you to turn away from focusing on yourself and to surrender to God's call for your life?

Are there areas in your life that you do not want to surrender?

Have you ever felt like an "elephant" as you have entered a new culture?
Have you been in situations where you saw others behaving like elephants in ministry?

Read Matthew 16:24–26.
Spend time in prayer, listening to what the Lord might be asking of you.

Invitation 3

From Guilt to Gratitude

As we came home, strong thanksgiving filled our hearts, thanks and praise unspeakable for the little lives safe in our nursery ... —and oh, from the ground of our heart we were grateful that He had not let us miss His will concerning these little children.

—Amy Carmichael, *Lotus Buds*[1]

We've followed on this long journey,

The road has not been smooth

But we've come, because we want to know more.

We've seen you work your wonders,

The blind receive their sight, and the lame they dance for joy.

Could it be that you will bring our freedom?

We sing glory, glory, glory to the King who comes to save,

riding on a gentle donkey. Is it you who've come to reign?

We sing glory, glory, glory to the King who comes to save,

riding on a gentle donkey. Is it you who've come to reign?

—"Glory to the King"[2]

Feelings of guilt can be even more paralyzing than fear, for they can become a prison where we feel trapped. But just as we are invited to lay down our fears and surrender ourselves to God, we are also invited to offer our guilt to the Lord. Whether it is guilt about past (or current) sins, guilt about being wealthy while so much of the world lives in poverty, or guilt for things that may or may not be our responsibility, God invites us to release our guilt so that we can experience the freedom that comes from choosing to follow Jesus and receiving a call to partner with him in loving the world.

---

1 Carmichael, *Lotus Buds*, Kindle ed., 991.

2 This is an excerpt from a song that Yosiah and I wrote during Holy Week in 2019.

By accepting Jesus's sacrificial death and trusting in the hope of his resurrection, we are washed clean and become *new creations*. Our resurrected lives in Christ should overflow with gratitude for what Christ has done for us!

When we humbly recognize that God has poured out his love for us and the whole world, we will be eager to join him in loving the precious people who are part of that world, particularly those who have never had an opportunity to hear about Jesus's grace.

Amy invites us to open our hearts to the self-giving love of God and find our strength in his abiding friendship. When we rely on him for our sustenance each day, our lives will overflow with gratitude.

Asking Amy: *How can our lives overflow with gratitude?*

Creator of my individual days

All variously distinguished, each is good

Distributed by Thee; my gratitude

Bestir; awaken praise.

Look back I dare not, knowing what I know;

O great Forgiver, flow

Over my yesterday; and my to-day,

Let it be clear and precious. I commit

Its outgoings to Thee: Lord, hallow it.

—Amy Carmichael, "Exalted and Ordinary Days"[3]

Some people in Amy's day considered her to be too extreme. During the early years of Dohnavur, some other missionaries and Indian Christians tried to force Amy to leave India. They could not understand her decision to wear Indian clothes, her desire to eliminate the segregation between Indians and Europeans, nor her battle against the temple system. As Elisabeth Elliot puts it, "She was a thorn in their sides."[4] Historians and missionaries today might also pass judgment on Amy: Why did she never take a furlough? Once she moved to India, why did she never return to Europe? Was she controlled by feelings of guilt, which kept her from allowing herself to travel back "home"? Why did she take in hundreds of children? Why didn't she live a more "balanced life"?

---

3 Carmichael, *Made in the Pans*, Kindle ed., 1427.

4 Elliot, *Chance to Die*, 198.

In reading Amy's many books, I have never gotten the sense that she felt guilty for being raised in Ireland by two loving parents who taught her about Christ. But she did believe that every child should have the gift of growing up in a loving home, with the opportunity to learn about Jesus. Her life was overflowing with gratitude to her Savior, and she knew that the good news of Jesus was too beautiful to keep to herself. For her, mission was very simple: if we really believe that Jesus offers us salvation from our sins, then we *must* share this news with others, for if we fail to do so, we are intensely selfish.

Amy challenged readers by asking poignant questions: "Do we believe in Calvary? What difference does it make that we believe? How does this belief affect the spending of our one possession life? Are we playing it away? Does it strike us as fanatical to do anything more serious?"[5]

Wanting to share the realities of "things as they are" in India, she invited her readers to journey with her—not because she wanted her readers to feel guilty, but because she wanted them to have a window into a different world. Amy wanted her readers to care about and pray for the children, the new believers, and the work in South India. She also wanted to inspire Christians in Europe to join in the mission movement, and she called on young people to come to the field, parents to release loved ones to the work, and churches to train and support workers with prayer and finances as an outpouring of gratitude for all that the Lord had done in their lives.

> *For Amy, mission was very simple: if we really believe that Jesus offers us salvation from our sins, then we must share this news with others.*

Because Amy believed that serving the Lord was a gift, she felt that the Christian life could be filled with incredible joy as we offer our lives to the Lord and receive from him in turn. She writes: "Oh, more than an Overweight of Joy is theirs who give to the Giving One. Mothers and fathers who have given, do you not say so? ... We fear to cause our dear ones pain. Should we not rather fear lest we hold them back from joy?"[6]

Amy sought to find hidden treasures everywhere in her life. Throughout her books, she paints powerful word pictures of the abundance of God's goodness in her life and the lives of the children at Dohnavur. She also praises God for the beauty of the creation around her in India—brilliantly colored flowers, intense rainstorms, tropical trees, majestic mountains, and

---

5 Carmichael, *Overweights of Joy*, Kindle ed., 732.
6 Carmichael, 734.

the crashing ocean waves provided living metaphors for the spiritual truths she shared. Amy was grateful for each breath the Lord gave her and each person that came into her life.

Contrary to the beliefs of some foreigners, Amy *did* value setting aside times for rest, but rather than taking furlough in Europe, she found a place *in India* where she could rest. For many years, she went into the hills of Ooty during the hottest time of year, where the weather was cooler. There was a lovely Christian woman in Ooty, Mrs. Hopwood, who became a spiritual mother for Amy.

As a servant of Christ in India, Amy also became committed to finding a way to rest *with* her Indian sisters in service and the many children in their care.[7] After praying for a place of rest for their community for many years, the community eventually purchased a beautiful property in the mountains, where they constructed simple buildings to serve as rest houses for the Dohnavur family. Amy wrote lovely stories about God's faithfulness throughout the difficult building process and how God met them in those mountain retreats. In *From the Forest*, Amy recalls these mountain escapades with gratitude: "There is so much sadness in the world, so many hearts ache, so many tears fall, it is rather wonderful to be away for a little while in a tearless world, left just as God made it … the calm strength of mountains is an uplifting, steadying thing, the pure clean joy of forests is precious, the ministry of rivers blessed healing."[8]

> Amy was grateful for each breath the Lord gave her and each person that came into her life.

Amy invites us to choose gratitude each day—to surrender our feelings of guilt, accept Christ's forgiveness, and then give our lives in grateful service to our king.

Lord, help us to accept the power of your resurrection in our lives. May our lives reflect the beauty and the freedom that you offer your children. Help us to overflow with gratitude in all we say and do.

---

7 "*We can never know an Eastern people—it is fallacious to imagine we do—while we find our chief recreation to be an escape from their companionship into the society of our fellow-Europeans … to be recreative, recreation need not draw us away from our people.*" Amy reflects in her little book *God's Missionary*, 43–44.

8 Carmichael, *From the Forest*, Kindle ed., 1686.

Living in Paradox

Here are some words from Ruskin, thought-out words, worth our thinking out ... "consider whether, even supposing it guiltless, luxury would be desired by any of us if we saw clearly at our sides the suffering which accompanies it in the world ... *luxury at present can only be enjoyed by the ignorant;* the cruellest man alive could not feast unless he sat blindfolded."

—Amy Carmichael, *From Sunrise Land: Letters from Japan*[9]

When I was twelve years old, I took a three-week trip to Central America with my parents and two younger brothers. As I stepped out of the airport into the parking lot, a throng of children wearing raggedy clothes and flip-flops rushed to surround me, stretching out their hands and pressing closer, begging for money. Though I had been born in Central America while my parents were serving as missionaries with Mennonite Central Committee, as I made this first trip back to the place of my birth, I felt acutely aware of my "white" complexion. And as all those hands reached toward me, so obviously a foreigner, my stomach clenched with guilt.

> I have come to realize that the question I need to ask myself is not, "do I feel guilty?" but rather, "How shall I live in response to these different realities?"

Years later, when I first moved to Jakarta as a young college graduate, I continued to struggle with feelings of guilt in the slum community where I lived as I witnessed inequalities and injustice day after day.

I have now been living with the urban poor for thirteen years and am married and raising two children in the slums. When my husband and I spoke at a mission conference in 2022 about our service in the slum community, a college student asked, "Do you ever feel guilty?" I answered, "Yes," for we constantly struggle with the reality that our neighbors were born into poverty while we have access to education, healthcare, and money. Through no fault of our friends—and no fault of our own—we were born into different realities. But over the years, I have come to realize that the question I need to ask myself is not, "do I feel guilty?" but rather, "How shall I live in response to these different realities?"

---

9 Carmichael, *From Sunrise Land*, Kindle ed., 211.

Several years ago, towards the end of our Christmas holiday, our family decided to pile into our car and head across Jakarta to a fancy mall, a rarity since the mall feels like a completely different world than the day-to-day reality in our slum community. But we were off in search of *Paw Patrol: The Movie*, as our boys are big fans.

After enjoying the film together, we were surprised to discover that this mall had something even better—a real dog park! This gated, AstroTurf playground for dogs had a yellow slide, a dog-sized swimming pool, and a dog salon next door. We watched in fascination as the wealthy paid for their dogs to get in—a sum equivalent to a day's wages for our neighbors. While our boys *ooohed* and *aaaawed* at the cute puppies, I struggled with the dichotomy of this totally different world existing just a short drive from my slum community.

I thought of my neighbors who survive by begging on the streets and all the hard-working women I know who could feed their families for two days with the cost of paying for one dog to enter the dog park. I also struggled with the fact that many of the people paying to get into the dog park probably identified themselves as Christians, since dogs are considered unclean to Muslims.

> *How are we to live in Christ's freedom amidst our consumeristic, narcissistic world?*

And I thought about our Indonesian interns, who told us that they grew up in churches that did not teach about God's particular concern for the poor. I wondered what these Christian dog-walkers might think about my friends and neighbors in the slums. To be fair, that trip to the mall also left me with a lingering feeling of guilt about the fact that we had spent $25 to see a movie in the theater—an amount that could pay the rent of a neighbor's home for a month.

Over the years, I have continued to wrestle with these and many other questions. How can we spend our time and money in ways that glorify God? How can we also accept the gifts of grace and rest? How are we to live in Christ's freedom amidst our consumeristic, narcissistic world?

As hands keep reaching out to me—just as the beggar children in Central America did so many years ago—I continue to wrestle with how to respond in love. But I have come to believe that Jesus wants to take away my feelings of guilt, because they paralyze me with the fear of mis-action. Instead, Jesus invites me to choose love, gratitude, and generosity.

Our neighbors in the slum community have taught me so much about living with gratitude and generosity rather than guilt and apathy.

One of my students, Siti, first came to our school when she was eleven years old. Because her family had moved back and forth between the slum community and their home village, her schooling had been interrupted, and so she was still at a kindergarten level, learning her ABCs. The nearby elementary schools had rejected her because she could not read, and so she joined our kindergarten program as an eager learner, who consistently arrived early every morning.

Each day, Siti came with her allotted snack money for the day, which she spent on snacks, candies, and little toys that she always shared with others. As the oldest in a classroom surrounded by five- and six-year-olds, Siti chose to share—even though her parents were garbage scavengers, and her snack money was precious. She was grateful for what she had and shared it generously—often with my youngest son. Siti, along with countless other children, are my teachers, who humble me with their gratitude for the littlest things and their open-handed generosity.

I have realized that the hands reaching out to beg from me are also inviting me on a journey of friendship. They are offering to hold my hand and lead me on a journey of learning from "the least" (Matt 25:40).

O Jesus, teach us to say "yes" to you every day. May we be so soaked in your lovingkindness that we overflow with gratitude—and may our gratitude lead us to live generously. We invite you to show us today where and how you want us to respond to your love.

Finding Jesus in Surprising Places

... when the mystery of the apparent victory of evil over good is overwhelming: even so there will be always a hush, a rest, a repose of spirit, as we stand by the Lotus-pools of life and seek in His Name to gather His flowers.

—Amy Carmichael, *Lotus Buds*[10]

The night before Desi was going to start first grade and her uncle was going to start high school, she went to sleep with butterflies in her stomach, a mix of excitement and nerves. As she lay in bed, she could see their new uniforms, which had been washed and ironed, hanging above their new shoes and backpacks. What would school be like? she wondered. Would she like it?

---

10 Carmichael, *Lotus Buds*, Kindle ed., 766.

In the middle of the night, Desi's mother shook her awake, calling, *Fire! Fire!* Desi followed her parents as they ran out of their house, her mother carrying her two-year-old sister, her father holding her hand. They rushed through the crowded alleyways in their sleeping clothes to the safety of the empty field that bordered their slum, where they joined hundreds of others who stood watching their homes and everything they owned go up in flames.

The next morning, Desi and her uncle could not go to school, as their uniforms had been lost in the fire. Now, she was homeless, living under an emergency tent provided by a relief agency.

As I sit with Desi fourteen years later, she cannot stop the tears as she remembers that traumatic night in July 2008 and her subsequent fear of fires. Each time she sees smoke or hears people yelling, "Fire," in her slum community, she grabs whatever she can and prepares to run.

I empathized with Desi, as I had also lived through a fire in the slum where I was living in October 2011. Over the past eleven years, I have talked to many moms in my community about their experiences with fires. Listening to Desi, I realized that the trauma she experienced as a child has been deep and long-lasting.

This has left me feeling guilty that my childhood was relatively trauma free. I never knew the pain of hunger or lived through a fire or natural disaster. And I also feel guilty that I have a bank account, health insurance, and access to good education for my own children. I struggle with the seeming incongruities and hypocrisies in myself, for I want to live simply and share generously, but I know that my own family *will* have a more comfortable life than Desi or any of my neighbors.

Although I know being *blessed* is a biblical concept, I struggle with the way we often use it in Western society. Many well-meaning Christians might say, "I was *blessed* with a good education." "I had the *blessing* of going on a cruise." "The Lord has *blessed* me with a healthy and loving family." "God has *blessed* my work abundantly."

While the Old Testament is full of examples of the Lord blessing faithful followers with gifts, material provisions, and wealth, I am not sure that *blessed* means what we think it does. After spending more than a decade living in a slum community in Jakarta, I think the above statements would be more truthful if we replaced "blessed" with "privileged." Because economic disparity is often connected with forces of global racism and colonialism, we cannot say that the rich are "more blessed" then the poor, but we can say that the rich are more "privileged" than the poor.

Jesus completely redefines our understanding of who is "blessed":

Then he looked up at his disciples and said:
"Blessed are you who are poor,
     for yours is the kingdom of God.
Blessed are you who are hungry now,
     for you will be filled.
Blessed are you who weep now,
     for you will laugh.
Blessed are you when people hate you,
     and when they exclude you, revile you,
     and defame you
          on account of the Son of Man." (Luke 6:20–22)

While some may spiritualize these words of Jesus, saying he only was talking about those who are poor in spirit, or hungry for God, or weeping for their sins, Jesus drew on these metaphors so that his listeners would understand his words both physically and spiritually. The poor are *blessed* because the kingdom *belongs* to them. Those who are hungry are *blessed* because they will *experience* fullness. Those who weep are *blessed* because they will be *comforted*.

For the millions of children growing up in poverty, encountering trauma upon trauma, I long for them to know that Jesus sees them, loves them, and receives them. I also long for Christians who come from wealthier backgrounds to stop posting #Blessed on their Instagram accounts and come alongside those who are struggling in poverty so that they can learn from them.

There are 1.4 billion people currently living in urban slum communities, and so we need to raise up a movement of servants of Christ who are willing to lay down their privileges and pick up the cross of suffering alongside the poor. Children who experience childhood trauma like Desi need us to care enough not just to read about urban slums, or pray (although praying is very important), or give money, but to release workers with

> *There are 1.4 billion people currently living in urban slum communities.*

training and passion to make the world a better place. Let us not just hoard our experiences, education, possessions, and time, for in the end, we might realize that we are like the rich fool, building bigger barns, but for what gain? (Luke 12:13–21).

As I seek to care for "the least" (Matt 25:40), I know that Jesus is inviting me to move beyond guilt so that I can meet him among those whom he describes as *blessed*. I do not want to be rocked to sleep by the comforts of wealth, for it is all too easy to be hypnotized by the consumer-driven lullabies that the world constantly sings to us, telling us to chase wealth and success and to build bigger barns. But Jesus tells his followers to seek the kingdom of God and to be generous and trustworthy with our earthly riches so that we can be entrusted with the abundant riches of his kingdom.

O Lord, forgive us for our complacency with the injustice all around us. Please give us new eyes to see you and willing hearts to obey you.

Room to Reflect

What stands out to you from Amy's story?

As you think about your own life, are there areas where you feel guilt?

Take a moment to reflect on things that you are grateful for today.

Now consider how God is inviting you to live more generously today.

Read 2 Corinthians 7:10.
Spend time asking the Lord to show you what areas of your life need repentance.
Relinquish feelings of guilt that are not from the Lord.

Invitation 4

From Control to Compassion

But look at it as we may, there is only one assurance which can entirely lift off the pressure of fear for the future. It is the assurance that just as the sanctifying, directing Presence of the Lord fills our present, so by His grace it will be in the future.

—Amy Carmichael, *The Continuation of a Story*[1]

I have crossed so many waters, only looking for your love

But now I'm tired, weak, and broken; Hope seems hard to grasp at all.

But now I've found you here: Waiting all this time

You are God my father. I've been O so blind.

Hallelujah, Hallelujah

Now you have found me by your grace.

Hallelujah, Hallelujah

I've been found by grace.

—From "Found by Grace"[2]

It is part of our human nature to want to feel like we are in control. And in Western societies, we can often enjoy the illusion that we are masters of our own destiny. But as road bumps and detours appear on our carefully crafted maps for the future, sooner or later we begin to realize that we cannot create or protect our "ideal life." As followers of Jesus, we are called to surrender to the Lord over and over again. Instead of holding our lives with clenched fists, we are invited to release control to the One who created us, casting all our anxieties onto the Lord, who cares for us (1 Pet 5:7).

As we learn from Amy's story, when we choose to follow Jesus, we are not guaranteed smooth sailing. In fact, for many people, choosing to follow Jesus leads to persecution and suffering. But as the Lord invites us into fellowship with him, he also instructs us to trust him with our griefs, burdens, and fears. Day after day, season after season, year after year, we are invited to surrender *everything* to God.

---

1 Carmichael, *Continuation of a Story*, Kindle ed., 1035.

2 This is an excerpt from a song that Yosiah and I wrote in 2013.

As we follow Jesus on this journey of downward discipleship, our journey will be much lighter if we humbly accept this invitation and relinquish control to God, allowing Jesus to transform our hearts with his *compassion* for those around us. The word *compassion* literally means "to suffer with." But when we suffer with and for one another, may we remember that the One who suffered before us has promised that he will never leave us or forsake us (Deut 31:8), but will be with us to the very end (Matt 28:20).

Asking Amy: *What can we do when we feel helpless and out of control?*

Hold us in quiet through the age-long minute

While Thou art silent and the wind is shrill;

Was ever a boat a wreck when Thou wert in it?

Can Spirit faint that waiteth on Thy will?

—Amy Carmichael, *Though the Mountains Shake*[3]

Amy believed that the Lord was leading her into new territory as they took in babies that were going to be dedicated to a life of service in the Hindu temples.[4] The first three "temple babies" brought joy and hope to Amy and her "Starry Cluster" community. But then, over the course of a few weeks, all three babies died of fevers. If this call was from the Lord, why had all three "temple babies" died? Why did the community have to suffer so much sorrow and pain in tending this hopeful and healing work?

As any parent or anyone who cares for children knows, we need to provide structure, guidance, and love for children, but ultimately, we are not in control. In Amy's context in the early 1900s, typhoid, dysentery, tuberculosis, and other infectious diseases were part of the reality of living in India. Because it was difficult to get medicines, these diseases often caused epidemics. During these years, the price and availability of food and materials was also greatly impacted by World War I and then World War II. In spite of these contextual realities, Amy chose to keep trusting that the Lord was in control. Casting her sorrows, griefs, and plans at the foot of the cross, she trusted Christ to comfort her.

After the community buried the third baby, Indraneela, Amy was overwhelmed by grief. In *Overweights of Joy*, she recalls:

---

3 Carmichael, *Though the Mountains Shake*, 1946, v.

4 Amy wrote, "To be a temple child means cruelty. It means a worse thing, even the turning of that child's mind from all that is good to all that is bad: it means killing the soul. And of all killings in the whole world, that is the worst." *From the Forest*, Kindle ed., 1692.

When we went back to the empty nursery, and folded up the babys'
little things and put them away, we felt as if we could not begin all
over again. But we were shown that what we had been through was
only meant to make us the more earnestly Persist. So we set apart the
sixth of each month, the date of our little Indraneela's passing, as a
Prayer day for the Temple children.[5]

For many years, on the sixth day of each month, Amy and her "Starry
Cluster" prayed earnestly for the release of children who were caught in the
temple system. They saw many answers to these prayers, often specifically
related to these days of prayer. "We have never had another Indraneela," Amy
writes, "but our empty nursery has been filled to overflowing. 'Impossible'
things have been done."[6]

Amy's vision was to raise up children who would dedicate their lives to be
servants of Christ and become agents of Christ's transformation throughout
India. As the years passed, the older girls became *Accals* ("older sisters"), helping
to raise their younger sisters and brothers. Some married young Christian men
and left Dohnavur while others chose to remain and serve at Dohnavur.

Amy's faithful coworker, Ponnamal, had been widowed at a young
age and was expected to live with her in-laws (as is the custom in India).
But in 1897, they finally permitted her to join Amy's band. Ponnamal
itinerated alongside Amy for eight years and then served with her as they
made their home in Dohnavur. After hearing a young girl comment to her
mother, "when I grow up, I will join the sister's band and wear beautiful
jewels," Ponnamal felt convicted and took off all her jewelry. At that
time, it was disgraceful for a woman in South India not to wear jewelry.
But Ponnamal set a striking example, which was eventually followed by many
of her Indian sisters. Amy remembers, "When we went home she took off her
jewels. How minute, how inoffensive the words appear now, set down in one
short sentence! But every syllable in them burned for us then."[7] Ponnamal
proved a faithful coworker, journeying with Amy for almost two decades.

As Dohnavur grew, the community discerned that it would be wise to
open a nursery in Neyoor, a town that was close to a hospital. The youngest
babies were cared for at the nursery in Neyoor so that medical help would be
easier to reach if the children became ill. In *Beginning of a Story*, Amy writes,
"Our brave Ponnamal, known to some by her translated name, Golden, is in
charge of the Neyoor nursery. She is God's golden gift to the work."[8]

---

5 Carmichael, *Overweights of Joy*, Kindle ed., 728.

6 Carmichael, 729.

7 Carmichael, *Ponnamal*, 1589.

8 Carmichael, *Beginning of a Story*, Kindle ed., 748.

As the entrusted leader of the Neyoor nursery, Ponnamal had many young nurses, new converts, and older women under her leadership. Describing Ponnamal, Amy writes, "Through all the difficulties incidental to such work, through severe strains, and in times of stress that test the stuff of which the soul is made, her faith and courage and utter love have never failed. We do thank God for Ponnamal."[9] After three years, the community decided to close the nursery at Neyoor, and the sisters at Dohnavur were joyfully reunited with Ponnamal and the growing babies.

Ponnamal also supported Amy when her spiritual mentor, Mr. Walker, suddenly passed away in his early fifties (while he was traveling in India and Mrs. Walker was in England). The Walkers had no biological children and loved the Dohnavur children as their own, and over the years they became dear friends of the growing Dohnavur family. In August 1912, a telegram informed Amy of his death, a heartbreaking day, as he had been a source of tremendous wisdom and guidance.

Ponnamal walked with Amy through her grief. In *Ponnamal*, Amy remembers: "Then, when at last we were left to our grief … stripped as I verily felt I was at that moment of my strongest earthly stay, she [Ponnamal] said: 'It must be that you are meant to lean on God alone.'"[10] And indeed, in the years that followed, Amy would continue to learn to lean on God alone. Surrendering control, she chose to trust that God was walking with them, even through the darkest valleys. Amy writes, "So we went on. And to our astonishment—so foolish are we and ignorant—that which we had thought we could not do, we did, God being our Arm every morning."[11]

> *So we went on. And to our astonishment—so foolish are we and ignorant—that which we had thought we could not do, we did, God being our Arm every morning.*

Amy was led even further into the valley of the shadow of death when Ponnamal became sick a few months after Mr. Walker's death. For two and a half years, Ponnamal battled cancer and was cared for by Amy. Ponnamal experienced excruciating pain and had to endure several operations but did not have access to the medications we have available now. Even amidst the pain, she had a steadfast trust in the Lord. During this period of intense suffering, Ponnamal shared with Amy that she could hear music—sometimes voices and sometimes a melodious sound. Whenever she heard this music, she

9 Carmichael, 749.
10 Carmichael, *Ponnamal*, 1622.
11 Carmichael, 1623.

forgot her pain and could sleep for hours in peace. Amy writes, "It was as if she had bathed in the night in the waters of immortality, and been renewed."[12]

Ponnamal died in August 1915, three years after Mr. Walker's death. Amy did not know how she could go on, having lost her most trusted and loved colleagues. But the work at Dohnavur *did* go on, and Amy processed her grief by writing books about two beloved friends: *Walker of Tinnevelly* (1916), a detailed biography of Mr. Walker's life, and *Ponnamal: Her Story* (1918), a beautiful tribute to her sister in Christ. Amidst the daily responsibilities and pressures of life at Dohnavur, Amy made time to remember and honor her friends, and this sustained her in the ongoing work.

In the closing words of *Ponnamal*, Amy writes, "My story has been told. It goes out into a world spent with suffering, wounded unto death. But death is not the end, it is only another beginning, and that which makes life lovable and glorious cannot die, for Love is eternal."[13]

Over and over again, Amy reveals how she chose to trust God and to cast all her anxieties on him. She had no illusions that she was in control … she surrendered to her loving Lord. Rather than giving into despair as she passed through the valley of the shadow of death, she clung to the hope that death does not have the final word. This hope gave her the strength to live a life overflowing with compassion, sharing God's love with those around her.

———————

Dear Lord, help us choose to trust you. Help us to cast our anxieties at your feet. Teach us to trust that you are in control and that you will hold us, even through the darkest valleys of life.

Trusting God When We Cannot See

There is torture in the too persistent "Why?" There is torment in the questions that spring upon us from the blackness of second causes: "the dark enigma of permitted wrong" is terribly intense. And it faces us sometimes so nearly, and it lashes us with the sharpness of thoughts that are like whips … Beyond our utmost reach sweeps God's great thought-horizon. Sometime, somewhere, we shall understand, and even if we never might, it could make no real difference; we know enough of our God to know all must be well.

—Amy Carmichael, *Overweights of Joy*[14]

———————

12 Carmichael, 1628.
13 Carmichael, 1638.
14 Carmichael, *Overweights of Joy*, Kindle ed., 665.

Many mornings, I leave our house and head out of our slum at around six in the morning for a short jog. After crossing a busy intersection, I enter a gated community, where I feel safer running. Having run this route hundreds of times, I was startled one morning, during the COVID-19 pandemic, to see mountains in the distance. I had been living in Jakarta for a decade and never seen those mountains before, because the city's pollution had kept them out of sight.

Since that day, I have not seen the mountains again, but *I know they are there*. This metaphor reminds me to trust God through hard times. For even when I cannot see God's hand at work, I can trust that God is present—just like the mountains covered by pollution. One day, I will get to see more clearly.

I am constantly tempted to seek control. In school as a kid, that desire led me to get straight As—and also led to an eating disorder. In parenting, my desire for control can lead to angry, judgmental interactions with my children. Underneath my desire to control is anxiety, and if I am in control, I feel less anxious. But Jesus sings a different song over his followers: "… do not worry about your life, what you will eat or what you will drink, or about your body, what you will wear … do not worry about tomorrow, for tomorrow will bring worries of its own" (Matt 6:25, 34). Jesus invites us to surrender control and trust that the Lord is a good father who cares for his children.

And Peter invites us: "Cast all your anxiety on him, because he cares for you" (1 Pet 5:7). Instead of seeking to control, I can choose to cast my anxieties on Jesus. The Greek word for "cast" here, ἐπιρίψαντες (*epiripsantes*), is used only two times in the New Testament. The other instance appears in the Gospel of Luke, when Jesus is preparing to enter Jerusalem: "Then they brought it [the colt] to Jesus; and after *throwing* [*epiripsantes*] their cloaks on the colt, they set Jesus on it" (Luke 19:35).[15]

> Jesus invites us to surrender control and trust that the Lord is a good father who cares for his children.

I love this image. The disciples did not know what was coming, and the way that their master was choosing to enter Jerusalem did not align with their hopes. Why would Jesus ride into Jerusalem on a borrowed colt, which seemed lowly and meek? Why not lead a violent revolt against the Romans and march in on a huge warhorse? But the disciples trusted Jesus and chose to obey his odd instructions about finding a colt—and then they *cast* their cloaks upon it.

Taking the verse from 1 Peter and combining it with the story from Luke, I pray that I will continue to choose to *cast my life upon Jesus*. May I let him

15 Emphasis added.

lead me in this strange, unexpected way of journeying. May I allow him to transform my heart with compassion and love for those around me.

Back in college, one of my best friends and I decided to walk from Camden, New Jersey, back to our homes in Virginia—a distance of more than 270 miles (434 km), which took us two full weeks. This was one of the most profound experiences of my life, as we took no money, no packed food, and only one change of clothes each. We wanted to experiment with traveling at the pace of first-century disciples, one step at a time. Before we set out, we called churches along our route and asked if someone from their congregations might host us.

I learned a lot of things on that extraordinary journey, but I have continued to reflect on an observation my friend made as we were walking: "Going downhill is just as hard—if not harder—than going uphill!" We longed to be rolling along on wheels, so that we could have sped downward, but instead we had to keep walking, one foot in front of another—and going downhill hurt our knees more.

Along the way, we were welcomed into twelve different homes, and as we received (and depended upon) such gracious hospitality, the Lord tangibly taught us about trusting him—and traveling light. On our first homestay, the pastor and his wife fed us a beautiful dinner, including a dessert of fresh strawberries and a bar of dark chocolate.

Walking an average of twenty-five miles a day, we felt exhausted at times, as if we could not go on. The asphalt under our feet was hot and hard, but step by step we continued the journey. This was before smartphones, and we relied on printed Google maps to guide us. Sometimes unexpected roadwork led to detours that added miles to our trip. Day after day was an exercise in trusting God one step at a time.

But there were many gifts throughout those two weeks. Because we were walking, we experienced many things that people traveling in cars would miss: the amusement of a yard with large statues of elephants, the smell of wildflowers along the road, the intense relief of finally finding drinking water.

On the last evening of our journey, our host was a masseuse (who happened to work with my mom), and she lovingly cared for our tired, aching feet. I remember laughing in awe at God's goodness during this time—utterly overwhelmed by such an overflowing cup of grace and provision.

As the years have passed, this walking journey has remained with me as I remember the lessons I learned about God's goodness through strangers— along with the unforgettable truth that walking downhill is still hard work! Again and again, my friend and I sensed that we were being received and embraced by the body of Christ.

Living as a foreigner in Jakarta, I often feel that I am not in control when I am at the mercy of government officials—if I qualify for a vaccine, whether I will be granted a visa, if I will be able to re-enter the country when I return from a trip abroad. Whenever I encounter these powers outside of my control, I am given the opportunity to practice trusting the Lord to open a way.

In 2019, our family was preparing to go to the USA on furlough. We had already purchased our tickets and were excitedly packing and planning, but my passport needed a stamp—an exit and re-entry permission slip. My husband had attempted to start the process early, arriving at immigration months in advance to apply for the re-entry permit, but the officials turned him away, saying it was too early. A month later, Yosiah returned, but was told that the office was under renovations and so they were not processing anything. A month before our anticipated departure, Yosiah tried for a third time. They accepted the application, but said the system was backed up from the renovations, and there would be a longer processing time than normal. We held our breath and surrendered my passport to the Lord. I wondered if I would be able to get on the airplane with my family.

A week before our scheduled departure the following Monday morning, Yosiah spent day after day running from one office to another, encountering obstacle after obstacle, until he finally learned that the entire country's immigration system was experiencing a computer error. Over the course of that week, Yosiah met many people from multiple other islands, who were all waiting in the Jakarta immigration office to try to pay bribes for their visa applications.

On Friday, we asked friends in Indonesia and around the world to pray for a miraculous release of my permit, and that afternoon, before the offices would close for the weekend, Yosiah returned to the immigration office. Refusing to pay the suggested bribe, he sat praying and waiting, and was surprised when he received a WhatsApp message from a different immigration office, saying that my payment had been processed and he could pick up my passport! Yosiah said goodbye to the dozens of others still waiting, giving thanks in his heart to God for working miraculously to release my permit. As he rode his motorcycle to pick up my passport, he praised the Lord for enabling us to board the airplane together on Monday.

This experience has taught our family a profound lesson about trusting God. When we are not in control, we are invited to trust the Lord and to cast our anxieties on the One who cares for us. Though a layer of fog or smog might be obscuring our view, we can trust in the God of the unseen mountains.

O Lord, forgive us for the times we have failed to rely on you. Help us in our times of unbelief, when we struggle to maintain order and seek to control everything. Teach us today what it means to surrender and to cast our lives, once again, upon Jesus.

Bringing Our Laments to the Lord

"All is windy about us now," Ponnamal wrote from the midst of the trial. "But the wind will not last always. The waves beat into our boat; but when the Lord says, Peace, Be still, they will lie down. Let all your prayer for us be that we may rest in the will of God while the wind lasts."

—Amy Carmichael, *Gold Cord*[16]

As we drove into our neighborhood after being away for the weekend, we noticed yellow flags marking the streets, which in Indonesia announces that there has been a death in the community. As we neared our street, we saw the final yellow flag, and my heart started beating as I wondered who had died.

We were shocked and shaken when we learned that a forty-three-day-old baby had died, just after his family marked his first forty days of life by shaving his head and cooking special food to share with all the families on our street. We did not know the family well, but the baby's mother, a sixteen-year-old girl, had attended one of my prenatal classes.

When I visited the family after the birth, the baby had seemed to be a healthy newborn. We wondered if his death had been caused by respiratory problems (the mom had smoked throughout her pregnancy and had smoked in their tiny house after her son was born), or if he had not gotten enough milk and died of malnutrition. The family's neighbors gossiped that they had watched the baby get smaller and smaller. Both the mom and the grandma said they had nursed the baby, but neighbors claimed that they had only seen the baby drink sweetened condensed milk. The truth is probably in between all those possibilities. My heart grieved for the tragic, seemingly avoidable, suffering and death of this baby boy—and for the poor, young mom who had already borne and buried a child.

> *Living as a foreigner in Jakarta, I often feel that I am not in control.*

---

16 Carmichael, *Gold Cord*, 74.

We see many so yellow flags in Indonesia and have watched our neighbors grieve the deaths of children, fathers, mothers, and grandparents taken by illnesses and accidents. So many of these deaths seem premature and heartbreaking. Our neighbors know that this is the reality of life in poverty, and so they walk around the community with cardboard boxes, gathering donations to help with burial costs. Even those who make their livelihoods from begging, scavenging, and garbage collecting share their meager earnings to help these families in need. I am always touched by these holy offerings.

The news is often filled with yellow flags as well, for Indonesia is on the Pacific Ring of Fire, where earthquakes, tsunamis, and other natural disasters are frequent. In 2018, an earthquake in Sulawesi that registered 7.4 on the Richter scale left over four thousand Indonesians dead.[17] My husband, Yosiah, heard firsthand from friends about the liquefaction of households and families as the ground literally opened up and swallowed whatever was there. Less than three months later, in December 2018, a small tsunami killed over two hundred people at our favorite beach location. I felt a shock as I realized that *we could have been there!*

More recently, the whole world was flying figurative yellow flags during the COVID-19 pandemic, and we collectively experienced the uncertainties that come with chartering the unknown territory of a new disease. We mourned and experienced fear as we watched the world spin out of control—and recognized that *we* are clearly *not* in control.

During my thirteen years among the urban poor in Jakarta, I have often felt that there is *too much* noise, *too much* heat, *too many* people, *too many* illnesses, *too many* underage marriages, *too many* divorces, *too many* parents abusing their children, *too much* injustice and pain, *too much* death, and *too many* yellow flags. I have experienced floods, multiple hospitalizations of our children and in-laws, anxiety attacks, cancer in my family back home, and many team struggles. Many days, everything seems hopeless and gray.

> *Many days, everything seems hopeless and gray.*

As I write this book, the community where we live has experienced yet another fire. Though neighbors fought together to contain the fire, over sixty homes were engulfed by the flames. A dozen firetrucks and many firefighters helped keep the fire from spreading further, but they arrived too late to save the many shacks that were already smoldering. After the initial hours of shock and panic, I find myself seething with anger and grief. Why, O Lord, do the poor suffer so much? Why do these families, who make their livelihoods by

---

17 Sangadji, "Central Sulawesi Disasters Killed 4,340 People."

picking through the trash of the wealthy, have to suffer yet another trauma? Why did these neighbors have to lose their homes—the poorest shacks in the community, built on top of the old community garbage dump?

The morning after the fire, we take a walk with our students, and they take our hands and guide us around the remains of the houses. "My house is gone," one girl says with a laugh, "I don't have any other clothes." In moments like these, I am reminded why we live here, but it is not an easy thing to love well. To look on suffering crowds with our Lord and to share his compassion is painful. It hurts us, just as it hurt our savior. It would be much simpler to choose a different way of life, hiding away from this raw human suffering. But when Jesus "saw the crowds, he had compassion for them, because they were harassed and helpless, like sheep without a shepherd" (Matt 9:36).

I picture the face of my student who lost her house in the fire and now has no clothes, and my heart aches with grief. But we do not face these hardships alone. We have a shepherd who promises that he is "the good shepherd. The good shepherd lays down his life for the sheep" (John 10:11). And as we walk through dark valleys, listening for his voice, we can trust that he holds our hands and walks with us.

Choosing to follow Jesus will not protect us from suffering. Many people who believe in Jesus have died of cancer, in car accidents, and of COVID-19. But as followers of Christ, we cling to the hope that Jesus is stronger than the storm—that at his word, all will be made right. For now, the winds blow, and the waves beat against our boat, but we can trust that Jesus is with us—and we can choose to cast our burdens and anxieties onto him.

———————

O Loving Savior, we believe that you join us as we weep for the brokenness we see all around us in this hurting world. When everything feels like it is too much for us to handle, we trust you to carry us through as we seek to live into your vision of shalom for the world.

Room to Reflect

What stands out to you from Amy's story in this section?

As you reflect on your own life, where do you recognize an unhealthy desire for control?

How is God inviting you to cast your anxieties on the Lord?

How do you sense God inviting you to grow in compassion for this broken world?

Read Philippians 4:6–7.
Reflect on how you have experienced the peace of God in the midst of difficult seasons.

Invitation 5

From Mammon to Manna

Our needs are supplied as Elijah's were, the children would tell you if you asked them. God sends His ravens. We have no provision made for us except what we share with the birds and the flowers; but it has never failed us.

—Amy Carmichael, *The Beginning of a Story*[1]

What has this to do with a peasant from Galilee?

Who taught that simplicity sets us free?

Who calls to all—"Pick up your cross and come with me."

Consumers can never be followers,

Focused on self, not sacrifice.

The narciss-sticks[2] of religion,

Dangerously lulling us to sleep.

Lies of safety and security,

Blinded eyes that cannot see.

O, Jesus, come and set us free.

—From "Consumer Church"[3]

As we follow Jesus in this journey of downward discipleship, God is inviting us to transform our view of money and physical possessions—along with the ways that we spend our time, talents, and energies. Though this may be an uncomfortable topic, if we are inviting Jesus to be the Lord of our lives and hearts, he must also be Lord over our finances.

---

1 Carmichael, *Beginning of a Story*, Kindle ed., 750.
2 Selfie sticks in Bahasa Indonesia are literally called, "Tongsis" (Tongkat Narsis).
3 This is an excerpt from a poem I wrote in my journal on 2 December 2022.

In many of Amy's books, she shares about her philosophy of *never asking* for money. Instead, Amy and the Dohnavur family took all needs directly to the Lord *in prayer*. This continues to be a radical and countercultural approach to ministry.

Jesus invites his followers to seek first the kingdom of God, but this seems much easier said than done. How can we tangibly choose to seek things of eternal value instead of directing our life course on the fast track to economic success? How can we avoid getting sucked into the consumeristic, narcissistic culture around us? How can we trust God to provide our *manna* each and every day?

These questions will frame our reflection on the invitation to journey from *mammon* to *manna*.

Asking Amy: *How will the Lord provide?*

The work has been a revelation of how many hearts are sensitive and obedient to the touch of the Spirit; for sometimes help has reached us in such a way and in such form that we could not but stand and worship, awestruck by the token of the nearness of our God.

—Amy Carmichael, *Lotus Buds*[4]

Amy lived long before debit cards, credit cards, or international transfers could be made through online banking over a cellphone. The late 1800s and early 1900s were difficult times financially for many people, but Amy trusted that the Lord would provide for her and the large family at Dohnavur.[5] When asked about her greatest need, she always answered, "Prayer." She refused to fundraise or ask people for money, and she did not authorize anyone to do so on Dohnavur's behalf. She simply believed that God would provide.

> Jesus invites his followers to seek first the kingdom of God, but this seems much easier said than done.

As Amy explains in *The Beginning of a Story*, "We rely upon the verses which assure us that our Father knows our needs, and we take it that with such a Father, to know is to supply."[6] The community at Dohnavur lived very simply, eating mostly rice and curries like their Indian neighbors.

---

4 Carmichael, *Lotus Buds*, Kindle ed., 868.

5 From 1895 to 1925, Amy received some money from the Church of England, as she was commissioned by the Anglican Church of England Zenana Missionary Society (CEZMS). However, the Dohnavur Fellowship then became its own entity and was no longer under any mission agency. Kommers, *Triumphant Love*, 430.

6 Carmichael, *Beginning of a Story*, Kindle ed., 750.

The exception was for the youngest babies, who required more expensive milk, condensed milk, and nutritional supplements.

All of the Dohnavur buildings were built and sustained by unsolicited donations, which came from around the world as people read about the work and felt moved to give. The buildings used for worship, nurseries, hospitals, school rooms, and dormitories gradually grew and expanded over the years as the Lord provided donations. There were also countless expenses for Dohnavur's growing needs, such as medicines, educational fees, clothing costs, and food. There were often travel fees related to rescuing the girls that joined them, as many of the babies and children came from distant parts of India.

The mailman often served as a "visible raven" for Amy and the rest of the community, delivering letters that contained money orders, cheques, and even rupees. Amy recorded many examples over the years of praying for a specific amount to meet a specific need—and weeks or months later, a letter arrived with that exact amount and a note designating that the gift was to be used for that particular need. Often the letter told of the donor feeling impressed at a *specific* time to give that amount. And while the mail system took weeks to deliver the gifts, Amy believed that God was in control and would provide in his timing according to his "good and acceptable and perfect will" (Rom 12:2).

> Amy recorded many examples over the years of praying for a specific amount to meet a specific need.

But Amy also knew that sometimes the community would need to go without things that they were accustomed to having. When World War I hit Europe, the ramifications reverberated all the way to Southern India. Inflation sent the price of many staples skyrocketing, and many of her supporters also spiraled into financial difficulties. But Amy continued to place her trust in God to sustain them through these years of scarcity. Her book *Nor Scrip* specifically details how the Lord provided for Dohnavur in financial ways throughout these difficult times. Though she was hesitant to share these things in writing, an old friend convinced her, "You ought to tell it.... It is keeping back something that belongs to Him if you don't."[7]

Amy shares story after story of the Lord's faithfulness in providing for the ministry at Dohnavur: "Thus almost visibly and audibly has the Lord, from whose hands we received this charge to keep, confirmed His word to us, strengthening us when we were weak, and comforting us when we were sad with that innermost sense of His tenderness which braces while it soothes."[8] In times when hardly any donations arrived and inflation kept the price

---

7 Carmichael, *Nor Scrip*, Kindle ed., 1724.
8 Carmichael, *Lotus Buds*, Kindle ed., 940.

of basic necessities out of reach, the Lord continued to sustain Dohnavur through what Amy called, "the Baskets." Recalling how Jesus had fed five thousand and there had been twelve baskets left over, she trusted that the surplus of previous years could sustain them until more donations arrived. Amy testified, "When the war ended not a workman or a coolie had been kept waiting a day for his pay, not a child had ever hungered, all twelve nurseries which had been our dream in 1913 were built and filled, a wall nearly a mile long was built, the Forest place was found and bought, and a house was built up there ... we poured from our pot of oil, and as we poured, more came to pour, according to the custom of the Lord."[9]

Amy firmly believed that if the Lord willed something, he would provide the finances. If the finances did not arrive for some particular building project, then the Lord's hand was not in it—at least not at the time. "Never once in fifteen years has a bill been left unpaid. Never once has man or woman been told when we were in need of help; but never once have we lacked any good thing."[10] Amy's stance on praying for God to provide was often a tangible testimony to the Hindu and Muslim community around Dohnavur. Many witnessed how the Lord provided for Dohnavur during those hard years and so gave glory to God.[11]

> Amy's stance on praying for God to provide was often a tangible testimony to the Hindu and Muslim community.

As others joined the work over the years, Amy's views on money continued to guide the community. The *Accals* ("older sisters") and *Sitties* (literally, "Mother's younger sister") who joined the ministry surrendered all earthly goals of chasing after wealth, often leaving behind a life of economic security in order to serve the Lord and the temple children they had rescued. As Amy writes, "There is absolutely nothing attractive about it. It is not 'honourable work,' like preaching and teaching. No money would have drawn these workers to us. Work which has no clear ending, but drifts on into the night if babies are young or troublesome—such work makes demands upon devotion and practical unselfishness which appeal to none but those who are prepared to love with the tireless love of the mother."[12]

---

9 Carmichael, *Nor Scrip*, Kindle ed., 1756.

10 Carmichael, 1733.

11 Amy wrote five books specifically detailing the faithfulness of the Lord in providing financially for the Dohnavur Fellowship: *Nor Scrip* (1922), *Tables in the Wilderness* (1923), *Meal in a Barrel* (1929), *Windows* (1937), and *Though the Mountains Shake* (1943).

12 Carmichael, *Lotus Buds*, Kindle ed., 927.

Dear God, thank you for the amazing testimony of your faithfulness in providing manna in the wilderness for Amy and the community at Dohnavur over many years. Help us learn to trust you more with all of our needs.

Giving More than Money

There, in that crowded, hot little room, a sense of the unequal distribution of the Bread of Life came over us. The front rows of the Five Thousand are getting the loaves and the fishes over and over again, till it seems as though they have to be bribed and besought to accept them, while the back rows are almost forgotten. Is it that we are so busy with the front rows, which we can see, that we have no time for the back rows out of sight? *But is it fair? Is it what Jesus our Master intended?* Can it be really called fair?

—Amy Carmichael, *Things as They Are*[13]

In 2012, about a year after my teammates and I were evicted from our first slum community, I was visiting the home of a new student in a makeshift shack at the furthest edge of the slum. I was surprised when some children brought Mina, a woman I had not seen in over a year, to see me. Mina had been my next-door neighbor before I had been evicted, and she had come searching for me, and these children had led her through many winding alleyways to find me on the far edge of this community.

As we walked back to my house, chatting amicably, I was a bit suspicious that she had come looking for me because she needed money. Mina (and many other neighbors in our slums) have often seen everyone on our team as walking dollar signs. While living next to her, we had tried to be good neighbors without becoming ATMs. But now, a year after we had been evicted from that slum, she had come looking for me—so that she could ask for money. I struggled, wondering how I should respond. *When is it okay to give and when is it wiser to not give?* I gave her a small amount to cover her transport home, but I did not give the large amounts she was asking for.

As Christians, our relationship to money can be extremely challenging and has caused much damage and pain throughout history. Countless books have been written about this subject, particularly in the context of cross-cultural ministry.

---

13 Carmichael, *Things as They Are*, Kindle ed., 399.

I once thought that by choosing to get rid of my possessions in the States and moving into a slum, I would suddenly be freed of the love of money. I had idealized visions of interacting with people who were physically poor, imagining that those with fewer possessions would be free of the love of money. And in many ways, my adventure of moving into a slum in another country has been freeing, and the physically poor have taught me a lot about how to hold things with open hands, be generous and hospitable, and give out of poverty.

But the truth is that *mammon*, which is the Greek word for money, property, and treasure, entices *everyone*—not only the rich. And Jesus said very clearly, "You cannot serve God and wealth [*mammon*]" (Matt 6:24b).

Jesus also taught his disciples to pray, "Give us this day our daily bread" (Matt 6:11). Another translation says, "Give us our food for today" (CET). In this prayer, Jesus is teaching us how to pray for God to provide *one day* at a time. The Jewish followers who were listening to Jesus would have remembered the stories of God providing manna in the wilderness for their ancestors. We are not called to store up wealth in bigger and bigger barns (Luke 12:16–21), but to trust God to provide enough manna for one day—and then the next. If the Israelites gathered more bread than they needed for one day, the manna would become infested with worms and rot (Exod 16:20).

Wealth entangles, strangles, and chokes spiritual growth. In the parable of the sower and the seed, Jesus describes seed that "fell among thorns, which grew up and choked the plants, so that they did not bear grain" (Mark 4:7 NIV). In explaining this third type of soil, Jesus teaches his disciples that the farmer is sowing the word of God, and though the seed sown among thorns starts to grow, "the cares of the world, and the lure of wealth, and the desire for other things come in and choke the word, and it yields nothing" (Mark 4:19).

Since moving to Jakarta, I have come to realize that wealth is not only about my physical stuff, but also how I view *my* time, *my* schedule, and *my* space. Do I live in a way that is open to interruptions, open to God's invitations and the Spirit moving? Or do I try to micromanage every moment of my day?

I have learned so much about what it looks like to be generous with time from my next-door neighbor, Ibu Gusti. Though Ibu Gusti had her own family, she started to care for a widow in our neighborhood, Nenek, after her health started to decline. Nenek had spent many years caring for her mentally ill grandson, whose parents had passed away. When Nenek became ill, her grandson would wander the streets for days at a time, leaving Nenek home alone. Every day, Ibu Gusti made time to visit Nenek, care for her, change her diapers, and bring her food. One night, when the streets in our slum began to flood, my husband, Yosiah, helped Ibu Gusti bring Nenek to our school in a garbage cart, as the school was on slightly higher ground and so it was a safer space for her to be.

As Nenek slept on the floor of our school building, I felt convicted by the generosity and care that Ibu Gusti had offered Nenek for so many months. Though Ibu Gusti was not a follower of Jesus, she was more Christlike than me! With barely enough money and food to feed her own family, she chose to share what she had with Nenek and to trust that God would provide for her family. I have learned so much by watching how she holds her possessions and time with open hands, always willing to share the little she has with others.

> *Perhaps God will ask with tears, "Why did you hold so tightly onto the talents and time I entrusted to you?"*

My husband Yosiah has also learned about generosity from our neighbors. One afternoon, as he was driving along the bumpy roads in our community to run an errand, he passed a very old lady carrying a heavy load. She looked lost as she made her way slowly into the slum, but he was in a hurry, so he did not stop to help her. His errands took him back and forth through our slum, and he passed this unfamiliar lady two more times. Finally, on his third trip—close to home—he saw that *another grandmother* had stopped to help this heavily laden grandma. Together, they carried her heavy sack to a nearby bench and sat down to talk.

Yosiah felt ashamed. Why had he not stopped when he first saw her struggling? Why hadn't he asked if she needed help? Too often, we realize after the fact that we are just like the priests and Levites in the parable Jesus tells in Luke 10 about the Good Samaritan. We pride ourselves as we read that story, nodding our heads and saying, "Yes, we will go and do likewise. We will be like the Good Samaritan." But how often we walk by those who need help because we are too busy, too scared, or too worried that we do not have the proper resources to help the person in need.

But the gifts we offer are acceptable according to what we have—not according to what we do not have (2 Cor 8:12).

God will not ask us why we did not provide homes for all the homeless people in the world. But perhaps God will ask us why we did not share our talents, resources, education, time, and lives to help a specific person who was near to us and needed our assistance at a particular moment in time. Perhaps God will ask with tears, "Why did you hold so tightly onto the talents and time I entrusted to you? Why were you so afraid? Did you not realize that *I* needed you?"[14]

---

14 In the parable of the sheep and the goats (Matt 25:31–46), Jesus tells those on his left (the "goats"), "Truly I tell you, just as you did not do it to one of the least of these, you did not do it to me" (Matt 25:45).

Lord, we repent of our love of mammon. May we not be like the foolish man who built bigger and bigger barns, only to die in his sleep. [15] *Instead, may we trust in you, the God who provides just enough manna for each day.*

Trusting God in Times of Scarcity and Plenty

So we continue as we began, asking only the One in Whose hand are all supplies, and the oil in the cruse does not fail. As we pour it out it comes. It is very simple but at times very awesome, for it brings the Lord our Master near and causes us afresh to recognize Him as practically, not just theoretically, in charge.

—Amy Carmichael, *The Continuation of a Story*[16]

"Yosiah, are you all right?" our neighbor, Bapak Gusti, asked as we sleepily answered our cell phone in the middle of the night. We were stunned by his next question, "Are you in jail?"

We assured Bapak Gusti that Yosiah was *not* in jail and we were out of town so he could attend school.

Unfortunately, Bapak Gusti had been tricked by cell phone scammers and had already transferred a hundred dollars to help "post bail" for Yosiah. We were touched that Bapak Gusti had been willing to pay such a large sum to help us, but we were saddened that he had been tricked—and angry that these manipulative scammers had taken advantage of him and so many other innocent people.

The love of *mammon* is the root of all sorts of evil. But how sneaky is the love of money!

We see this every time we go on furlough. We pack up our designated suitcases, filling one with spices that we hope will last us six months and at least one with gifts. We hug our friends goodbye and then embark on a cross-cultural excursion—from the slums to the Land of Plenty. Even sitting on the airplane feels like a different world than our normal life.

The silverware on the plane, do they reuse it? I wonder. What about the blankets? For many international fliers, airplane food is a dreaded experience, but for us it seems like an extravagant feast. Cheese! Butter! Chocolate! An unlimited choice of drinks—juices, teas, coffee, milk, and so on. It is as if everyone is screaming, "Welcome to Wealth." Not to mention the personal

---

15 Luke 12:13–21.

16 Carmichael, *Continuation of a Story*, Kindle ed., 1028.

electronic devices, which bring an unlimited supply of entertainment, available at our fingertips, while we careen through the atmosphere between continents. What a strange time we live in.

Right before we left for furlough in December 2022, our youngest son's best friends gave him birthday gifts—a purple, stuffed rabbit, an electronic alien with a helicopter on his head, and a funny game that involves sticking plastic swords into a pirate that jumps up like a jack-in-the-box. Our son loved these gifts, and I enjoyed watching him sit on the floor with his buddies, playing with these new toys. I was touched by their generosity, as their dads all worked as garbage collectors, and I knew that their families did not have much money to spare.

> *It is as if everyone is screaming, "Welcome to Wealth."*

When we arrived in the States, we jumped right into Christmas celebrations with friends and family, and the abundance of food, toys, books, and cookies left us all feeling overwhelmed. All too quickly, the presents that had meant so much in Indonesia were now just gathering dust in a drawer. It is so easy to get comfortable, to forget what we have learned from living in simpler environments. It is too easy for the treasures to get lost in the abundance.

During our furlough, my older son heard me talking with my dad about skiing and piped up, "Are you going cross-cultural skiing?" I laughed, as he had apparently heard the term "cross-cultural" more than he had heard "cross-country."

But, yes, I realized, our family is cross-cultural skiing.

This delicate dance between different worlds can be exhausting and frightening as well as beautiful and easygoing. But as followers of Christ, we are called to *bridge* these different worlds—and to fill our lives with the real wealth of Christ's kingdom.

I need Christ to help me see the treasures that are all around me in my life in the slums of Jakarta, and I am still learning how to trust God to provide for our family. But in our journey of cross-cultural skiing, I believe that God is present, helping us learn how to navigate our way between such different worlds.

Whether we are living in the Land of Plenty or the wilderness of our daily life in the slums, I want to trust God to provide just enough manna for our family each day—that I do not need to hoard, gathering more than my share. I also want to remember and give thanks for all the times that the Lord has been faithful in providing for us. As I live with gratitude for God's past faithfulness, I can continue to trust him to be faithful in the future.

As we prepared to return to Jakarta, I prayed that I would have eyes to see all the ways that God is providing manna for our family—rather than dwelling on all the comforts that we were leaving behind in America.

When the Israelites were wandering around the desert, it did not take them long to forget God's miraculous intervention and provision in their lives and to start complaining about the things they missed from their time of slavery in Egypt. Though their lives had been hard, and they were oppressed by the Egyptians, they groaned about missing the cucumbers!

> We remember the fish we used to eat in Egypt for nothing, the cucumbers, the melons, the leeks, the onions, and the garlic; but now our strength is dried up, and there is nothing at all but this manna to look at. (Num 11:5–6)

Oh, Lord, help us to be grateful for the small gifts you so generously give to us, often through the hands of our friends and strangers.
Help us to see the ways you provide miraculously—and not to compare your manna to the mammon we have left behind.

Room to Reflect

What new things stand out to you from Amy's story?

Has the Lord ever provided for you in a way that seemed miraculous at the time?

Read Matthew 6:24.
In what ways do you find yourself trying to serve God and mammon?

Read 1 Timothy 6:10.
How have you seen the love of mammon lead to evil in your own life?

Ask God to teach you about manna. Pray for God to help you trust him for your *daily bread.*

Invitation 6

From Poverty to Praise

Oh for a return to the days of the beginning of the Acts of the Apostles, to obscurity, and poverty, and suffering, and shame, and the utter absence of all earthly glory, and the winning of souls of a different make to the type thought sufficiently spiritual now!

—Amy Carmichael, *Things as They Are*[1]

For a king born a babe

for the world he came to save.

Hay and mud, blood and tears,

what an entrance.

You could have chosen the palace:

Robes and trumpets, gold and bliss.

But this is You, born a babe in a manger.

You are our King, and You Shall Reign.

—From "Psalm 72 Remix"[2]

As we learn to rely on God to provide our daily manna, we will still feel overwhelmed and scared at various times in our lives—for we are only human, not superheroes—and the pressing needs and realities of life will often feel heavy. But as Amy's life and writings demonstrate, Christ's disciples are called to follow a countercultural path, choosing to live in hope and to praise God, even though our circumstances may be incredibly difficult.

Whether we acknowledge it or not, poverty is a reality in our world today, and the disparity between the rich and poor is growing at an alarming rate. Newsfeeds bombard us incessantly with distressing stories, which numb us to the pain of those who are suffering. Amy's witness and years of faithful work in India can guide us as we seek to live humble lives of discipleship and follow our Savior by loving and serving those who are in need.

---

1 Carmichael, *Things as They Are*, Kindle ed., 479.
2 This is an excerpt from a song that Yosiah and I wrote for Christmas in 2018.

In this section, we will reflect on the things that sustained Amy through her decades of work in India.

Asking Amy: *How can we be sustained through seasons of suffering?*

But God is the God of the waves and the billows, and they are still His when they come over us; and again and again we have proved that the overwhelming thing does not overwhelm. Once more by His interposition deliverance came. We were cast down, but not destroyed.

—Amy Carmichael, *Lotus Buds*[3]

Throughout Amy's life, she experienced different forms and degrees of poverty, but she believed that choosing a life of relative material poverty was part of her decision to follow Jesus. Earthly riches had no pull on her heart, for she had devoted herself to a life of loving service and the way of the cross.

Because Amy and her band were trying to change a practice that was deeply entrenched in Indian society (the dedication of young girls to the temple system), they were like David fighting against Goliath. Throughout this long struggle, Amy relied on prayer as her strongest weapon.

Whenever Amy and others at Dohnavur became aware of a specific child who was in danger of being dedicated to the temple system, they would intercede for that child. They often saw doors miraculously opened as one child after another was brought to them. Sometime a prayer was not answered immediately, but came months or even years later,[4] and Amy would remember when the community had prayed specifically for a child and how that intertwined with the child coming safely to Dohnavur. In some situations, a conflicted guardian would be debating in one room about whether the child in their care should be given to the temple or to Dohnavur, and Amy would have teammates praying in an adjacent room, waging battle with unseen forces until the guardian made a decision—many children were rescued because of this type of prayer.

> Even though they were fighting against a system of incredible darkness, they continued to believe that Jesus had the victory.

Prayer for Amy and the community at Dohnavur always led to praise. Even though they were fighting against a system of incredible darkness, they

---

3 Carmichael, *Lotus Buds*, Kindle ed., 860.

4 "For prayer is not emotion, it is a traffic between earth and heaven, a 'commerce of love.' Our ships set sail for heavenly shores; they do not return empty, it is impossible that they should … We think in terms of time: God thinks in terms of eternity." Amy writes in *Plowed Under*, 136.

continued to believe that Jesus had the victory and that one day all would be made right. Throughout Amy's books, she made hundreds of references to the word "praise," and she praised God even when the community's prayers were not answered in the way she hoped. She believed that God was worthy to be praised, even when children died of unexplained illnesses—and even when she spent her last two decades as an invalid, stuck in bed.

The intense material poverty, spiritual poverty, and poverty of health that Amy encountered in her missionary work brought her to her knees in prayer, as she believed that fervent and devoted prayer was the key to the battle they were fighting. This posture of prayer led her into praise, as she also believed that God deserved praise for every victory as well as every obstacle. She could even write, "But praise God for forlorn hopes, for impossibilities, for blank walls rising straight up overhead. Such things are challenges …"[5]

Amy knew that the community could not accomplish anything on their own strength but needed to rely on God to lead and guide them. Fighting the temple system was seen as a "foolish waste" in the eyes of the world—and even in the eyes of some Christians at the time. She received many letters with the question, "To what purpose is this waste?" But in spite of this resistance, Amy continued to hear a different voice, the voice of her Savior, saying, "Take this child away (away from the terrible Temple) and nurse it for Me."[6] She poured out her life in response to the voice of Jesus, following him in a way that was difficult for many people to understand.

Amy also challenged those around her—as well as readers today—to discover the sacredness of the ordinary. As she writes in *Lotus Buds*, "The Secular and the Spiritual may not be divided now. The enlightening of a dark soul or the lighting of a kitchen fire, it matters not which it is, if only we are obedient to the heavenly vision, and work with a pure intention to the glory of our God."[7] She led the community at Dohnavur to put this belief into practice by praising God with their whole lives. This meant that the women on

> *Amy challenged those around her … to discover the sacredness of the ordinary.*

duty changing the babies' diapers had no less an important task than those leading worship in the church on Sunday morning. The women sent out on missionary journeys were no more important than the girls carrying water jars or preparing food in the Dohnavur kitchen. The secular and the spiritual

---

5 Carmichael, *Continuation of a Story*, Kindle ed., 1007.

6 Carmichael, *Lotus Buds*, Kindle ed., 940.

7 Carmichael, 938.

could not be divided, as our entire lives belong to the Lord, and worshiping God should encompass all the different spheres of life.

In the tiny yet powerful book *If*, Amy wrote, "If by doing some work which the undiscerning consider 'not spiritual work' I can best help others, and I inwardly rebel, thinking it is the spiritual for which I crave, when in truth it is the interesting and exciting, then I know nothing of Calvary love."[8]

Amy believed that the Lord was worthy of all praise and that whatever material, physical, relational, or spiritual poverty the community encountered, the Lord would carry them through. She joined with all creation in singing praise to the Creator and often found living metaphors from the woods to share with others.

One day, while staying in the community's forest home, Amy noticed the beautiful butterflies that appeared to have gold on their wings. She reflected, "For the earth is full of God's riches, and He puts these things in it for our comfort perhaps, knowing some of us are often short of the other gold which is so useful for the present. He who has gold to spare for pupae and butterflies' wings, say the little clear voices that sound from all creation, will find enough for us to do all He means us to do."[9]

Lord, help us to choose to praise you, even in the midst of our difficult experiences. Help us to meet you in our moments of heartbreak and whenever we feel overwhelmed by our own needs and the needs of those around us.

Clinging to Christ's Hope in Times of Disappointment

Work among children always seems to me to be a sort of undermining of the fortress: a work presenting little immediate result, but certain to produce one in the future.

—Amy Carmichael, *From Sunrise Land: Letters from Japan*[10]

In tropical climates, some things grow very quickly. Our next-door neighbor planted small saplings, and within a few years, they were as tall as me—and just a few years later, they were as tall as their house.

---

8 Carmichael, *If*, 39.
9 Carmichael, *From the Forest*, Kindle ed., 1670.
10 Carmichael, *From Sunrise Land*, Kindle ed., 210.

Yet often when Yosiah and I plant things in our slum community, they quickly die: chickens eat vegetable sprouts, children tromp down plants, or goats come along and decimate every living thing. We have had very little luck growing anything!

Amidst the suffocating poverty and cruelty all around us, we often wonder if we can possibly bring any lasting change into the world. Do the seeds we plant have any chance of growing, or will they be snatched up or crushed down before there is any real growth? I think of the hundreds of children we have taught at House of Hope over the years and how few make it through middle school or high school. Many children drop out in later grades because they lack school fees, or do not have uniforms, or they have too many absences from traveling home to their family's villages for weddings, funerals, or illnesses. Other times, they drop out because they experience bullying or the teachers are too strict. And many girls drop out to get married.

> *We often wonder if we can possibly bring any lasting change into the world.*

The seeds of love and care that we strive to plant in these children's lives seem miniscule when compared with the negative influences they have experienced. On hard days, I wonder what difference a few hours with us a day can make.

When I feel overwhelmed by the tragic needs around me and my inability to *do* enough to alleviate the pain of my neighbors, I try to remember that it is not my responsibility to make everyone happy or to solve the complexities of urban slum communities. When I recognize my own poverty and inadequacy, I am freed to put my trust in Jesus as the Savior—rather than myself. And as I receive from Christ's abundance, my focus on poverty begins to shift to praise.

Amidst despair and hopelessness, I can choose to root myself in praise. This is not some sadistic song, like the legend of Nero strumming on his fiddle as Rome burned, but rather the choice to refocus my sight on the Lord. There have been many seasons during my years in Jakarta when I could not find words to pray, but I could sing, and the music of praise and lament became my prayer. And on days when I could not find the strength to sing, the music of my brothers and sisters washed over me, and I let them sing for me.

During these difficult seasons, I have also drawn strength from Scripture. As Paul writes in his second letter to the Corinthians:

> "My grace is sufficient for you, for power is made perfect in weakness."
> So, I will boast all the more gladly of my weaknesses, so that the power

of Christ may dwell in me. Therefore I am content with weaknesses, insults, hardships, persecutions, and calamities for the sake of Christ; for whenever I am weak, then I am strong. (2 Cor 12:9–10)

While our family was on furlough in the United States, my sons enjoyed watching the birds in my parents' backyard—brilliant red cardinals, bright blue jays, and even dull brown sparrows. While my sons have seen many colorful birds in cages in Jakarta, they have rarely observed birds in the wild. We all stood transfixed at the window, watching the birds fly back and forth.

As we watched the birds together, I thought of Jesus's words in the Sermon on the Mount, where he instructs his followers not to worry or be afraid of poverty, saying, "Look at the birds of the air; they neither sow nor reap nor gather into barns, and yet your heavenly Father feeds them. Are you not of more value than they?" (Matt 6:26).

Yet the forces of evil continue to numb us or to leave us seething with rage, at a loss for how to respond. For the world is full of poverty, and until Christ returns, there will be children who do not have access to education, proper healthcare, or safe living situations. But each day, we are invited to pause from our frantic attempts to fix the messes in the world and to choose to root ourselves in worship, declaring that Jesus is the king of the coming kingdom.

As we seek his kingdom, we plant seeds of life by caring for the poor, fighting injustice, and teaching the children entrusted to us. We sow, often while weeping, but we cannot force the growth, and so we live in trust that one day, we will reap with joy (Ps 126:5). As the disciples learned when Jesus multiplied the bread and fed the five thousand, we need to choose to believe that with Jesus, there will always be *enough*—and sometimes, there will even be baskets left over!

When our next-door neighbor pruned the trees that had grown up as tall as his house, he cut off a large branch with the radius of a cantaloupe and laid it by the side of the field next to our house. For over a year, I had to step over it whenever I walked to and from the field. Then one day, our neighbor picked up this seemingly dead log and planted it in front of our school. Within a few weeks, green sprouts began coming out of the top, and as the weeks passed, I watched it grow before my eyes into a tree.

> Yet the forces of evil continue to numb us or to leave us seething with rage.

Every day, as I watched its rapid growth, I praised God for bringing life out of something I had thought was dead. Though the things we plant may die, God can bring forth astounding growth in the people and places for which we have lost all hope.

———————

Dear God, help us to trust you with our disappointments and failures. We entrust our whole lives to you, acknowledging that you see and understand things that we cannot. May you surprise us with growth and life in unexpected ways!

Discerning the Sacred Task of the Doula

Look in with eyes anointed with the sympathy of Jesus. Look out again—look upon the fields—and then, oh! we plead with you, look up—"Lord, what wilt Thou have me to do?" Yours in the Fight, Looking for the coming of the Conqueror.

—Amy Carmichael, *From the Fight*[11]

While I was in training as a birth doula, a midwife from our neighborhood knocked on our door one night and asked if I wanted to attend a birth with her. I quickly got my children to bed, kissed my husband goodnight, and then walked through the slum to find the home of the woman who was in labor.

When I arrived, the midwife explained that the woman was only dilated one centimeter, and so it would likely be a few hours until the birth. I held the mama's hand as I introduced myself, and she gave me a weak smile as she kept breathing through her contractions. Then a knock called the midwife to the front door, and she returned to explain that she needed to attend to another patient and would be back soon. I hoped she would not leave us alone for long.

After an hour or so, I could tell the mama was beginning to push, and so I said, "Don't push! You are not fully dilated, and your midwife is not here!" Then I called to a neighbor and asked her to run and fetch the midwife.

But the woman kept bearing down, and as she groaned and strained, I lifted up her batik skirt—and found a beautiful baby girl! I placed the baby on her mama's stomach, then grabbed a blanket and covered them both.

A few minutes later, the midwife waltzed back in, surprised to see the baby, who was crying and healthy. I returned home, glowing with the adrenaline of being present for such a quick delivery.

I long for my work in the mission field to be like that swift and easy delivery. I long for my Muslim neighbors to birth a movement of Jesus followers without me really doing anything! I long to be present for the miraculous, to see something beautiful happen quickly. While faithful Christians have witnessed such radical conversions, I have come to believe

———————

11 Carmichael, preface, *From the Fight*, Kindle ed., 224.

that many conversions—like labor—involve a long, slow, painful process. Our role is to serve as birth doulas[12]—accompanying, journeying alongside, patiently being present with our friends, encouraging, witnessing, humbly giving suggestions, and sharing about our own journey with Jesus. But we can never force change or force people to meet Jesus.

Our friend Ibu Sifa was slowly bleeding to death, similar to the woman in Scripture who bled for twelve years before being healed after she touched the fringe of Jesus's garment. Ibu Sifa's husband had four wives (which is acceptable but rare in our slum community), and he supported his family by gathering recycling and picking through the trash. Ibu Sifa was too weak to help with scavenging, so one of our teammates took her to the hospital, where she learned that she had stage four cervical cancer. Because the family had no money, paperwork, or insurance, Ibu Sifa returned home to wait for death.

Our team visited her frequently over the next months and tried to bring her comfort, praying with her, sharing stories about Jesus (*Isa Al-Masih*), and giving her an mp3 player with New Testament audio recordings. While she did not miraculously recover, she told us that she believed in Jesus. As our team visited her and prayed with her, we often wondered why God would allow our first "believer" to die. Why would her years of suffering in poverty end in months of excruciating pain? Though she was buried with Muslim rituals and surrounded by her Islamic community, we trust that Jesus heard her cries and ushered her into a new life, where she will no longer suffer.

> We often want shortcuts in missions, to wave a magic wand and watch God fix everything immediately.

We often want shortcuts in missions, to wave a magic wand and watch God fix everything immediately. But there are no shortcuts in a life of compassion, which literally means, "to suffer with." As ministers of the gospel in places of intense darkness and despair, we are called to be doulas in both birth and in death, hopeful that we will one day celebrate as we welcome people into new life in Christ. But suffering with others is not easy, and it will require much sacrifice.

When the intense poverty in Jakarta leads me to despair, I must remember to fall on my knees and worship Christ for the new life he is continuing to bring into the world each day. We are not responsible for saving the world, for God already sent his son to save the world. Rather than trying to fix the

---

12 In *Subversive Mission*, Craig Greenfield says that our role as cross-cultural workers is to be "midwives." I have borrowed this idea, replacing "midwife" with "doula." See chapter 8 of *Subversive Mission*.

world, God is inviting us to journey alongside others and to bear witness to Christ and his power wherever we are.

Not long before we left Jakarta for our furlough in December 2022, I heard a commotion at the end of our street. Yosiah went to investigate and learned that Bibi, our neighbor, had been thrashing like a snake on the ground, possessed by a demon. Yosiah went to visit Bibi after neighbors helped her return to her house, and he found her quietly resting. But later that evening and the following day, the demon returned and attacked her multiple times. She spoke in strange voices, her eyes were glazed over, and she had a physical strength that was not her own.

Her family moved her to her sister's house, where she could receive more care, and Yosiah and I, along with a Bible school intern, visited her. We prayed that the Lord would protect us and give us courage to pray for our friend, who was suffering this demonic attack.

When we arrived at the house, we saw dozens of pairs of sandals at the front door. Many of our neighbors were present, along with Bibi's extended family—great aunts and uncles, along with the family patriarch—who had been summoned from her home village to dispel the demon.

We held Bibi's hand and asked permission to share, even though we were not Muslims. They welcomed us to share as friends and part of their community, so we told them about Jesus, *Isa Al-Masih*, and how he had power over evil spirits. I asked permission to share a story from Scripture, and then I read the story of Jesus casting out the legion of demons from the suffering man in Gerasene (Mark 5:1–20).

Sitting on the floor in that small shack in my slum community in Jakarta, I felt overwhelmed with the sacredness of the moment as I read from the gospel of Mark to my Muslim neighbors. *This is why we live here,* I thought, *so that I can share the Lord's love and care with these neighbors!* We explained that we could pray for the demon to leave, but that Bibi would need to be filled with a greater power—or the demon might return. When we asked Bibi if she would like to study more stories of Jesus together, she shook her head no. Ironically, her father nudged her and said, "Yes, you should. You should."

So we prayed for Bibi, and she grew calm, but then the attacks returned, and suddenly her two sisters started screaming from an adjacent bedroom.

Yosiah, the intern, and I each prayed for the three possessed women. Though words failed me, I began to sing, "There is power in the name of Jesus." After about an hour, things calmed down and we returned home—unsure of how things would resolve with Bibi and her family.

Although we will often face despair, singing songs of worship can help us cling to the belief that, in time, Christ will restore all things. Our battle is not against flesh and blood, but will lead us into realms we cannot understand (Eph 6:12–13). When we choose to praise or lament in the midst of despair and discouragement, we take small steps that anchor us in God's love—as we trust God's provision for our lives and for the whole world.

Lord, we long for the day when you will bring the miraculous birth of transformation into our community and into broken communities around the world. Though we are tired of our long labor, we trust your timing, and we join with creation in groaning for the day when all will be made right.[13]

Room to Reflect

What new things stand out to you from Amy's story?

Where do you sense poverty in your own life—physical, emotional, or spiritual? Invite God to meet you in this place.

Read Hebrews 13:15–16. How might the Lord be asking you to praise him this week?

Invite one or two friends to join you in praising God while lamenting for a difficult situation.

---

13 Rom 8:22.

Invitation 7

From Asking *Why?* to Welcoming the Word

Hammer this truth out on the anvil of experience—this truth that the loving thoughts of God direct and perfect all that concerneth us; it will bear to be beaten out to the uttermost. The pledged word of God to man is no puffball to break at a touch and scatter into dust. It is iron. It is gold, that most malleable of all metals. It is more golden than gold. It abideth imperishable forever.

—Amy Carmichael, *Gold by Moonlight*[1]

Come to me tired, burnt out and busted

Broken and weak, searching for cures.

I am your Father, please let me name you

Drink from my spring and thirst no more.

Here's the truth, you are mine

Beloved and beauty, I love you.

Here's the truth, you are mine

I poured out my blood to save you.

—From "Names"[2]

On our journey of seeking to follow Jesus, questions will inevitably arise in our hearts. It is important to remember that questioning is not a bad thing, and the process of growing and deepening in faith often comes through difficult seasons of uncertainty. But we must not get lost in our questioning, especially by endless refrains of asking, "Why?" *Why did this happen? Why didn't that happen? Why did God allow this?* Such haunting "whys" can drown us, smothering our hope and blinding our eyes from the joy and beauty that is still present around us.

---

1 Carmichael, *Gold by Moonlight*, 48.
2 This is an excerpt from a song I wrote during Ramadan in August 2011.

As we have been learning from Amy, her journey in India was not easy. But because the Lord continued to sustain her through many years of crisis and pain, she abounded in joy and hope. How can we live within such a juxtaposition? How can suffering and hope exist simultaneously? Though poverty and the distressing realities of the temple system surrounded Amy, she still chose to praise God. And hand-in-hand with praise, she remained deeply rooted in Scripture and in Christ, the Living Word.

As we seek to follow Jesus in our own lives, we will need to acknowledge that there is so much we will never understand. Many realities will not make sense to us. But we are invited to root our hearts in God's Word, where we will find the sustenance to carry on—even when we do not understand what is happening around us.

Asking Amy: *What can we do with our questions?*

This work for the children, which seems so strangely full of trial of its own (as it is surely still more full of its own particular joy), has held this bitterness for us, and yet the bitter has changed to sweet; and even now in our "twilight of short knowledge" we can understand a little, and where we cannot we are content to wait.

—Amy Carmichael, *Lotus Buds*[3]

What kept Amy going for over fifty years in India? How did she weather foreign teammates dying and leaving the field? How could she carry on when it often seemed like the evil they were battling was winning? How did she handle the despair of knowing that for every child they rescued, thousands more were dedicated to lives of temple prostitution? And how did she arrive at peace in her bedridden life, when she became unable to serve as she had before? The force that sustained, strengthened, and encouraged her, granting her peace and joy that passes all understanding, was the daily bread of reading Scripture, being nourished by the Word of God.

Amy's books are steeped in Scripture, and Bible verses are woven throughout her letters and writing—sometimes with references, but often without. She clearly loved her Bible (including the apocrypha, which she frequently quoted), and she taught her Dohnavur family to do the same. Daily quiet time was set aside for everyone, including young children. Times of communal worship, Bible reading, and prayer were also built into the rhythms of the Dohnavur community. Amy knew the children's limits, however, and insisted that services remain fairly brief. But Scripture, Amy believed, was to be considered daily food—they all needed it in order to carry on.

---

3 Carmichael, *Lotus Buds*, Kindle ed., 820.

Amy's deep faith and years of studying Scripture enabled her to write eloquently and live into a theology of suffering. She did not believe that Scripture promised a life of ease, but that following Christ would lead us to inevitable hardships. She believed that if our Lord's feet were pierced and bleeding, then ours should be, too. Since Jesus had scars, we, as his followers, would have scars as well. Amy did not seek suffering for its own sake, but saw it as an expected outcome of following a crucified Lord.

For Amy, there was a real battle being waged, and followers of Christ were invited to join in the struggle against the powers of darkness, which were entangling young children in tight webs of evil. Amy felt led by Christ to rescue children from those webs and offer them a different future as beautiful children of God. But over the years, Amy learned not to get lost in the continual "whys?" *Why did God take this child? Why did this child not get rescued in time? Why did Ponnamal have to suffer and die?* Amy believed that she must surrender

> *Over the years, Amy learned not to get lost in the continual "whys?"*

such questions to the Lord and trust his goodness—even in bad situations. She chose to trust that God was in control, even when she could not see the final picture. She invited her community—as well as her readers—to choose to find hope in the promises of God's Word.

During times of struggle, Amy found particular strength in the psalms, the laments, and the promises of Christ's final victory, which enabled her to keep hoping. She writes, "Then, in spite of all that was said, all the verses we had ever read about God's doing impossible things came crowding into our mind. We could not give up hope. Together we waited upon Him to do the impossible."[4] Again and again, God answered her prayers—sometimes miraculously, but other times, the answer was not what she had been seeking. Yet she continued to trust that one day, all would be made right.

Amy was also sustained by her faith in the *living* Christ, who had called her on this journey and would not abandon her. She writes honestly of her struggle as she acknowledges, "For heart may faint and questions crowd, 'Is the Word true? Shall the faith stand? Is the work worth such woe as this? Can the day recompense the night?'" Yet her faith in Christ's presence is unwavering, for she concludes, "Christ walks with you even now while the flints cut sharp and the feet bleed."[5]

---

4 Carmichael, *Overweights of Joy*, Kindle ed., 551.

5 Carmichael, 619.

Although the feet may bleed, the path may seem difficult, and the questions may be haunting, Amy invites us to continue to surrender everything to the living Christ, the Word Made Flesh, who journeys with us. Inviting us to find our refuge in him, she writes, "As we rest our hearts upon what we know (the certainty of the ultimate triumph of good), leaving what we do not know to the Love that has led us all our life long, the peace of God enters into us and abides."[6] May it be so.

Lord, help us to follow you, even when the path is rocky, and our feet hurt. Carry us through these times with your Word. When we feel blown about and beaten by our circumstances, may your Word root our lives and be our strong anchor and home.

Recognizing We Need a Savior

Sometime, somewhere, we shall understand, and even if we never might, it could make no real difference; we know enough of our God to know all must be well... "[Jesus] answered," so the Tamil reads, "come to Me; I will cool your weariness." Not, I will answer your questions, but "I will give you rest."

—Amy Carmichael, *Overweights of Joy*[7]

Living in an urban slum is sometimes like living in a rural village, as neighbors have a strong sense of community and share life together in ways that are less common in wealthier neighborhoods. "I would never want to live in a gated community," our friend Ibu Gusti says with a laugh. "If I needed to borrow a bowl of spicy sauce, who could I ask?"

We also have the joy of having many animals around us, which is uncommon in other parts of this mega-city. Chickens wander the streets, pecking the ground for food. Sheep and goats wander by during the day, nibbling anything green they can find before their owners round them up and shepherd them home in the evenings. During each rainy season, the field near our house turns into a swamp, where beautiful white geese spend hours floating around in puddles, and our boys enjoy catching tadpoles and tiny frogs.

Having not grown up on a farm, I find all these animals intriguing and am happy to have them as part of our life here—albeit at a distance. When I watch the sheep that occasionally wander by our house, I think of the Bible passages

---

6 Carmichael, *Gold by Moonlight*, 21.
7 Carmichael, *Overweights of Joy*, Kindle ed., 665.

that compare humans with sheep, and I am humbled to admit that "All we like sheep have gone astray; we have all turned to our own way" (Isa 53:6).

Sometimes, we hear the sheep bleating and run outside to discover that one has gotten itself tangled in the soccer net on the field. They are incapable of getting out on their own, but I am reluctant to touch them because their matted coats are filthy, as they spend a lot of time picking for food from piles of garbage. But I also remember how Jesus calls himself "the good shepherd" and says, "The good shepherd lays down his life for the sheep" (John 10:11). And so I take a deep breath, and my sons and I head over to the soccer net to help set the tangled sheep free.

When I see newborn lambs, I am always amazed by their pure white fur as they go bounding after their mothers. But once, I saw a fuzzy white lamb atop a pile of smoldering garbage, caught in the springs of a burned-out mattress, and I began to weep. I remembered the passage in Matthew's gospel, when Jesus was travelling about all the cities and villages, "teaching in their synagogues, and proclaiming the good news of the kingdom, and curing every disease and every sickness" (Matt 9:35). Then Matthew says that when Jesus "saw the crowds, he had compassion for them, because *they were harassed and helpless, like sheep without a shepherd*" (Matt 9:36, emphasis added).

> *Most of these billion people will never have an opportunity to hear about Jesus.*

When I think of that pure white lamb on top of the garbage heap, I imagine Jesus seeing all the beautiful children here, who grow up on top of the city's rubbish, and having compassion on them for being *like sheep without a shepherd*. I imagine him looking at the *billion* people living in the slums in Jakarta and around the world and having compassion on them for being *like sheep without a shepherd*. I grieve that most of these billion people will never have an opportunity to hear about Jesus. For as Jesus acknowledged to his disciples in his time, "The harvest is plentiful, but the laborers are few" (Matt 9:37).

When I see such innocent beauty, surrounded by such ugliness, I can get stuck, asking, "Why?" *Why* do my friends back in America have homes of abundance, each decked out with enough books, toys, and resources to open a kindergarten program for a hundred slum children? *Why* do people have huge garages for their cars while people in slums are living under makeshift shacks? *Why* do wealthy people in Jakarta complain about the smell of smoke, unaware that it is their own trash burning? *Why* do so many of my students drop out of elementary school? *Why* do so many thirteen-year-olds in my neighborhood "choose" marriage? *Why* was I born with a blue passport that entitles me to an entirely different reality than my friends in Jakarta?

My list of "why" questions could go on and on. Each of us probably has our own list of "whys." Why do injustice and sorrow and pain exist?

Humans really are like the bleating sheep in my neighborhood, who occasionally get caught in the soccer nets in the field next to my house. We cannot free ourselves from the tangled mess we have made of our world. We desperately need a savior who will gently remove the cords that bind us so that we will be free.

When I get stuck asking, "why?," it is tempting to demand answers or get angry. But Jesus offers me a different path. After acknowledging to his disciples that "the harvest is plentiful, but the laborers are few," he gives them the following instruction: "therefore ask the Lord of the harvest to send out laborers into his harvest" (Matt 9:38, emphasis added).

Rather than drowning in questions or falling into despair every time I see a newborn lamb (because I know that soon enough, its clean, white coat will become stained with dirt), I can ask the Lord of the harvest to send more laborers into the field. This is an invitation to pray without ceasing. As a disciple of Christ, I can turn to Scripture, and I can trust the Lord, who is my Shepherd, to guide me to green pastures of truth and still waters of hope that will restore me and sustain me all the days of my life (Ps 23:1–3, 6).

> When I get stuck asking, "why?," it is tempting to demand answers or get angry.

When Jesus is in the desert for forty days, he rebukes the Tempter by quoting from Scripture: "It is written, 'One does not live by bread alone, but by every word that comes from the mouth of God'" (Matt 4:4).[8] When we choose to *ask* God to sustain us when we are flooded with uncertainties and living through a season of spiritual drought, God's Word will become our manna, our daily bread, our life-source.

Dear Jesus, be our life-source each day! Forgive us for trying to fill our hunger with fleeting things. Help us choose to be nourished by your Word. Calm our troubled hearts so that you can untangle us from the nets we have gotten ourselves caught in. You are our Lord and Good Shepherd, and we trust you to guide us through each moment of each day of our lives.

---

8 Jesus is quoting Deuteronomy 8:3: "He humbled you by letting you hunger, then by feeding you with manna, with which neither you nor your ancestors were acquainted, in order to make you understand that one does not live by bread alone, but by every word that comes from the mouth of the LORD."

Rooting Ourselves in God's Word

But though we would praise Him with our song, His Word alone is the cause of our sure confidence. The song may brighten the day's work, and lighten the very night, but nothing short of the Word of the Lord stands strong through everything. This battle is His. The victory was won on the Resurrection morning. Christ our King is King of the ages. Although we could not sing we would still go on.

—Amy Carmichael, *Overweights of Joy*[9]

"Would you like to read the Bible with us?" a friend asked towards the end of my last year of college. "The entire Bible, out loud, in one week?"

I am not sure where she got this idea (friends that were Korean missionaries, perhaps?), but I thought it sounded like an amazing adventure, and so we made plans, picked dates, and eagerly awaited the experience with several others.

We were excited to read the Bible as it was meant to be read … out loud, in community. The Torah (first five books of the Old Testament) is traditionally chanted to the religious community and the New Testament is a series of letters that were meant to be read or recited orally to a specific group of mostly illiterate people.

It took us six days (four days for the Old Testament and two days for the New Testament), reading aloud from morning until bedtime, with breaks for meals and sleep. We rotated reading, one chapter at a time, so that our voices would not get too tired. As we listened to others read, we drew illustrations and wrote down themes and words that stood out to us on a large roll of white poster paper, which slowly filled the living room as we responded artistically to each book of the Bible. From Genesis to Revelation, we read the stories that have become our faith heritage.

There is a beauty and a joy in hearing entire books at a time, an experience that I will never forget. While I still appreciate the value of spending time reading Scripture on my own, meditating on a few verses or chapters a day, our "Bible Week" taught me the importance of listening to God's word in community. I participated in a "Bible Week" reading for two years, and my friends have carried on the tradition numerous times while I have been overseas.

I was raised as a pastor's kid and grew up in a community that deeply loved Scripture. Having daily times reading the Bible and praying was encouraged by my faith community, Christian school, and my family. Growing up, we

---

9 Carmichael, *Overweights of Joy*, Kindle ed., 532.

moved many times, but my life remained anchored in Christ and the Bible. As I have made my home in Jakarta over the past thirteen years, I have been carried by continuing to root myself in Scripture. But living in a Muslim context has also stretched my understanding of God and Scripture—and how I interact with both.

The Bible is not only a book to be cherished and read, but points us *to the living Word*, who "became flesh and lived among us" (John 1:14). The word "live" literally means "to pitch a tent" among us. And following the living Word calls us to *pitch our tent* along with Jesus, who *pitched his tent* among us.

When we follow Jesus and desire to learn from him, every week can be "Bible Week" as we engage the *living Word* all day long. Because God has taken on flesh and come to dwell among us, our daily grind can become sacred. We not only find the holy in the pages of Scripture that have been entrusted to us, but we also find the sacred in humanity, who has been entrusted to create history. And Jesus told us that we can find him *specifically* when we interact with those who are poor and suffering.[10]

> These words are sacred promises that the Lord continues to breath to life in front of us.

In my limited experience, opening the Bible and reading it in a comfortable padded church pew is very different from reading the same words while standing in a garbage dump. But I need to believe that Scripture has something to say in this context. And over and over again, God speaks to us in this place—through both the written Word and the living Word.

One of my favorite Scripture passages before moving to Jakarta was from the prophet Isaiah:

> Do not fear, for I have redeemed you; I have called you by name, you are mine. When you pass through the waters, I will be with you; and through the rivers, they shall not overwhelm you; when you walk through fire you shall not be burned, and the flame shall not consume you. For I am the LORD your God, the Holy One of Israel, your Savior. (Isa 43:1b–3a)

These words have now taken on a whole new meaning to me. I have seen God's faithfulness, journeying with our family in this place—literally through fires and floods. These words are not just writing on a page, they are sacred promises that the Lord continues to breath to life in front of us. The Lord promises to be *with* us. He is our savior, *through the waters* and *through the flames*.

---

10 See Matt 25:31–46.

There are countless moments when the Lord speaks to us through interactions with the *living Word*, through meeting Jesus in our community. One day, I was visiting one of our students in her home. Her face was snotty, lice crawled in her hair, and her clothes were dirty. But I knew that I needed to love her and not shrink away from her hug. *This is how you might appear to me, too, you know,* I felt God saying to me. *You also were a mess. But I still embraced you. In the same way, you are invited to love these precious children.*

For years, we have longed to interact more intentionally with the youth in our community, but we felt stretched too thin as we were busy with the kindergarten and elementary school program. But about a year ago, my husband Yosiah invited a group of preteens in our neighborhood to hang out once a week. These boys have experienced fires, floods, evictions, and other traumas that are part of being raised in an urban slum. Many of them lack positive role models or father figures that can speak truth into their lives.

They studied a peace curriculum together—peace with self, peace between different ethnic groups, peace amongst different economic groups—and then they started studying Bible stories together. A similar group with preteen girls was also started by some of our teammates. Reading stories from Scripture with those who have never heard them before is a blessing, as our young friends are helping us see the stories with new eyes, and it is profound to hear the words of Scripture being read out loud by Muslim boys and girls in our slum community.

We invite the Holy Spirit to speak through the Scripture stories, showing more of who God is to our friends. One particularly relatable story with a surprising ending is the parable of the prodigal son (Luke 15:11–32). The teenagers listened carefully as Yosiah shared the tale of two sons, one obedient and one wayward. After squandering his father's wealth, the youngest son was full of shame, guilty by his own doing, and at his wits' end. He decided to return to his father. The logical outcome to this story should be rebuke and punishment for the youngest son. But the father shows us a different way. Yosiah shared with the boys how this is a picture of who God is: a loving father who is *longing to welcome us home*, with arms opened wide. We pray that this beautiful truth would take root in the hearts of these precious young people.

The Word of God is not only for us to read and study on our own, but it is a gift that we can share in loving, contextually appropriate ways. We miss out on so much when we only read the Bible with others who grew up going to Sunday school.

Jesus is not only our friend but is also our savior and master. Having seen his glory (John 1:14), Jesus calls us to follow him and worship him with our lives, trusting that our (imperfect) lives, actions, and words will introduce others to Jesus.

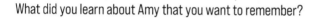

Dear God, we long and hope for the day when our neighbors will surrender their lives to your beautiful Word. As we wait for this time, help us to accept the invitation to surrender our thundering "Whys?" each day so that we can receive the peace that comes from being rooted in you, Jesus, the Living Word.

Room to Reflect

What did you learn about Amy that you want to remember?

What questions do you want to ask God? Write them down.

Spend time surrendering these questions to the Lord.

Read 1 Corinthians 13:12. Invite God to help you trust in him, who sees clearly and knows you fully.

Conclusion

We want that touch of God: "Touch the mountains, and they shall smoke."
That is why we write. For we write for those who believe in prayer—not in
the emasculated modern sense, but in the old Hebrew sense, deep as the
other is shallow. We believe there is some connection between knowing
and caring and praying, and what happens afterwards ... we stand on
the edge of the pit, and look down and tell what we have seen, urged by
the longing within us that the Christians of England should pray.

—Amy Carmichael, *Lotus Buds*[1]

While I was on furlough in America at the start of 2023, I had the joy of watching spring unfold. After years in Indonesia with year-round tropical weather, experiencing the contrast of winter and spring was a joy. The yellow daffodils blossomed, the scent of white dogwood flowers was in the air, and the warmer temperatures on walks and jogs brightened my days. It was during these months of rest that I penned most of this book.

My prayer is that this book would invite readers into a season of spring renewal—that the Lord would bring forth new hope in your hearts and lives as you consider what it means to follow Jesus on the path of downward discipleship. Many of us have been lulled into the comfortable slumber of winter and need to be awakened with a new vision and passion for following Jesus.

> *My prayer is that this book would invite readers into a season of spring renewal.*

May Christ's breath flow over all who pray to him, melting our cold hearts and equipping us for lives of sacrificial service.

With so many people in the world suffering and living without hope, Christians cannot remain asleep any longer. It is time for us all to grow, blossom, and spread beauty throughout the hurting world. As we turn our faces toward the Son, receiving warmth and life from him, may we trust God to give us the miraculous strength to continue—even when everything seems cold and dark, and we feel alone and misunderstood.[2]

---

1 Carmichael, *Lotus Buds*, Kindle ed., 825.

2 "If we take courage to expect, we shall have crushing disappointments sometimes, but often we shall find. And we shall tap deep wells. We shall discover a power and abandon of love to our blessed Lord Jesus that overflows our poverty of faith. Not the emotion of a moment, but the passion of a lifetime, this is what the Lord our God can effect, if only we rise to His thought. We ask far too little of men and women redeemed by the precious blood of Christ, and the smoky, smouldering life of many who might have been flames for Him, and the frigid and measured quality of service that they offer, is our sorrowful, just reward. But do we ask enough of ourselves?" Amy Carmichael, *Widow of the Jewels*, 91–92.

As we learned from Amy's story, God is faithful. Though he may call us into difficult places, he will not abandon us—but will sustain us, light the way, and carry us through whatever hardships we may face.

May Amy's long and faithful life of downward discipleship in India give each of us the courage to listen to the voice of Jesus, who is inviting us to follow him—even when the way is unexpected and difficult.

Like Amy, may we move beyond fear and accept the friendship that God offers us so that we can learn to love ourselves and experience the joy of cultivating new friendships with those around us.

As we remember Amy's story, may God give us the courage to surrender ourselves—our dreams, hobbies, ambitions, and even potential careers—and place everything at the foot of the cross as we wait patiently for the Lord to guide us.

Rather than being weighed down by guilt, may our lives overflow with gratitude, as Amy's did. In this world of immense disparity between the "haves" and the "have-nots," may we humbly acknowledge our privilege and surrender whatever we can so that we can live generously instead of greedily.

> Like Amy, may we have the courage to trust Jesus with the impossible.

When we find ourselves trying to control our lives and everything around us, may we hear Jesus's invitation to join him in having compassion on those around us. Like Amy, may we cast our anxieties on him, trusting him to lead and guide us in ways that are better than anything we could imagine ourselves.

And when the temptations of *mammon* surround us on every side, screaming for our attention and grasping for our allegiance, may we have the courage to trust God to provide our daily *manna*. May we remember how the Lord faithfully provided for Amy and the Dohnavur Fellowship, and may we give thanks for how God has provided for our own needs as well.

If our journey leads us through the wilderness, may we learn to trust that Christ will not fail us. When we feel the weight of poverty all around us and feel intensely aware of how little we are in the battle against evil, may we lift our voices to God in praise and lament. Like Amy, may we have the courage to trust Jesus with the impossible.

And when we wrestle with questions that leave us asking, "why?" in the face of all the brokenness in this world, may we learn from Amy to root ourselves in Scripture, trusting God to give us the strength to carry on, and trusting Jesus, the Living Word, to be our life source and our guide.

As we choose to follow Christ in this journey of downward discipleship, may we draw ever closer to God's heart.

Let the same mind be in you that was in Christ Jesus, who, though he was in the form of God, did not regard equality with God as something to be exploited, but emptied himself, taking the form of a slave, being born in human likeness. And being found in human form, he humbled himself and became obedient to the point of death—even death on a cross. (Phil 2:5–8)

Epilogue

Some of you, who are longing to live this life, still hesitate. There is no life in all the world so joyful. It has pain in it, too, but looking back I can tell you truly, there is far more joy than pain. Do not hesitate. Give yourselves wholly to your Lord to be prepared for whatever He has chosen for you to do.

—Amy Carmichael, *Candles in The Dark*[1]

On 18 January 1951, at the age of eighty-three, Amy Carmichael passed away at Dohnavur, her beloved home. She instructed that no stone be put over her grave, and so her community marked the burial spot with a simple birdbath. This seems very fitting, as Amy loved watching birds and taught all her children to treat God's creatures with gentleness and respect. On one side of the birdbath, there is a simple inscription with the date of her passing and the word, *Amma*, which is the Tamil name for "Mother." This is also fitting, as Amy was called "Mother" ever since the children began joining her in 1901, and Amy was a mother for hundreds of children over the years. Her legacy continues in the ongoing work of the Dohnavur Fellowship today.[2]

> From the beginning, Amy believed the Dohnavur Fellowship was a family rather than an orphanage or an institution.

From the beginning, Amy believed the Dohnavur Fellowship was a family rather than an orphanage or an institution. As she puts it, "And we all, Indian and European, men and women, live and work together on the lines of an Indian family, each contributing what each has to offer for the help of all."[3] By the time of Amy's death, there were over eight hundred people in this family.

Throughout Amy's decades in India, she worked tirelessly to help both women and children. She surrendered her entire life to the Lord, and the ripples of that decision have impacted hundreds of thousands of people throughout the world. From her early years serving the "Shawlies" at The Tin Tabernacle in Belfast, to her brief experiences in Japan and Sri Lanka, and through her faithful half-century at the southern tip of India, Amy's life

---

1 Carmichael, *Candles in the Dark*, 4.
2 For more information, visit https://dohnavurfellowship.org/.
3 Carmichael, *Though the Mountains Shake*, 292.

shines with the Lord's love. She believed that God called her, equipped her, and went before her as she continually surrendered her life to the Lord. As she writes with great confidence, "'God is gone … before thee.' *Hills and valleys*, every sort of roughness, what are they to the power of the King? Then let us cross our rivers, and fear not our valleys, though they be Giants' Valleys. For the Lord is gone before. Always and everywhere He goeth before."[4]

When Amy boarded the ship that sailed away from her home in Europe, never to return, she did not know what lay before her, but she trusted the One she believed had called her to follow him. In speaking of her faith, she writes, "If we *saw* the victorious issue of the fight, it would not be a fight of faith. If we *saw* the end of the road clearly and the reason why we are being led along this particular road, we would not walk by faith but by sight. Again and again the emphasis is on faith."[5]

If you found the stories in this book inspiring and interesting, I hope you will continue reading more about Amy. *Gold Cord* tells the story of the Dohnavur Fellowship in Amy's words and would be a great place to start!

Lord, thank you for the life of your faithful servant, Amy Carmichael. Give us the faith and courage to follow wherever you may lead us. Amen.

---

4 Carmichael, *Edges of His Ways*, 121. In this passage, she is referring to 1 Chr 14:15.
5 Carmichael, 108.

Appendix A: Journal Entry

Consumer Church[1]

Hundreds wait in lines,
Scanning codes,
High heels clinking on perfect tile floors.
Fancy clothes, freshly pressed,
Tattooed eyebrows and detailed makeup.
Like blind sheep,
Pushed forward, herded into the auditorium.

All eyes on stage—
Rehearsed music, precise technology,
Creating a One-Hour Experience.
Congregants check off the box,
Eager now to go mall shopping.

What has this to do with
A peasant from Galilee—
Who taught that simplicity
Sets us free?
Who calls to all,
"Pick up your cross and come with me."

Consumers can never be followers,
Focused on self, not sacrifice.
The narciss-sticks of religion
Dangerously lulling us to sleep.
Lies of safety and security,
Blinded eyes cannot see.

O Jesus, come and set us free.

---

1 Journal entry from 2 December 2022.

Appendix B: Songs

Glory to the King[2]

We've followed on this long journey,
The road has not been smooth
But we've come,
cause we want to know more.
We've seen you work your wonders,
The blind receive their sight, and the lame they dance for joy.

Could it be that you will bring our freedom? (2x)

> We sing glory, glory, glory to the King who comes to save, riding on a gentle donkey
> Is it you who've come to reign?

> We sing glory, glory, glory to the King who comes to save, riding on a gentle donkey
> Is it you who've come to reign?

We've seen you upset some tables
Reclaiming God's sacred space
And we cheered, but there are others here.
The leaders do not accept you,
They fear your power and words.
Now their cries are ringing in our ears.

Could it be that you will bring our freedom? (2x)

> They said "stop him, crucify him,
> The one who claims that he is Lord."
> They nailed our hopes upon the cross,
> All our dreams we thought were lost. (2x)

Could it be that you will bring our freedom? (2x)

> We sing glory, hallelujah to the King who rose again!
> Through your death you won the victory
> It is you Lord come to reign! (2x)
> Through your death you have bought our freedom
> Through your life you have brought our freedom.

---

2 Yosiah and I wrote this song during Holy Week in 2019.

I've Been Found by Grace[3]

I have crossed so many waters, only looking for your love
But now I'm tired, weak, and broken
Hope seems hard to grasp at all.

> But now I've found you here
> Waiting all this time
> You are God my father
> I've been O so blind.

> Hallelujah, Hallelujah
> Now you have found me by your grace.
> Hallelujah, Hallelujah
> I've been found by grace.

I have tried so many costumes,
Just to earn myself respect
But now I see it's all so useless
Cause you know it's all an act.

---

3 Yosiah and I wrote this song in 2013.

Names[4]

Garbage, trash, ugly, and worthless
Stupid and dumb, we are the poor.
Dark-skinned, and flat-nosed,
Nannies and waiters, singers and beggars
Here at your door.

> *Can't you see, these are lies*
> *These names that you carry*
> *They're not you.*
> *Can't you see, these are lies*
> *Your father has spoken the truth over you.*

Talented, smart, pretty, and handsome
Qualified privileged, we are the rich.
White-skinned, and long-nosed,
Doctors and nurses,
White-picket fence in our suburban bliss.

> *Come to me tired, burnt out and busted*
> *Broken and weak, searching for cures.*
> *I am your Father, please let me name you*
> *Drink from my spring and thirst no more.*

> *Here's the truth, you are mine*
> *Beloved and beauty, I love you.*
> *Here's the truth, you are mine*
> *I poured out my blood to save you.*

---

4 I wrote this song during Ramadan in August 2011. The "names" in the first paragraph are common phrases that my neighbors in the slum community used to describe themselves. In contrast, the "names" in the third paragraph are terms they used to describe foreigners. The words in italics are the Lord speaking truth over both sets of misconceptions.

Psalm 72 Remix[5]

He will defend the afflicted
among the people
And save the children of the needy
And he will crush down all the oppressors
O Yeah
He will endure as long
as the sun and the moon

He will be like rain,
Falling on the field
Showers watering the earth
O how we thirst
O how we thirst

> For a king born a babe
> for the world he came to save
> Hay and mud, blood and tears,
> what an entrance
> You could have chosen the palace
> Robes and trumpets, gold and bliss
> But this is You, born a babe in a manger
> You are our King, and You Shall Reign

He will deliver the needy who cry out
His people, all those afflicted
with no one to help
He will take pity on the weak
and the downcast
Save them from all oppression
and violence

He will rescue and redeem
Comfort and Restore
For precious is their blood,
precious is their blood
Precious in His sight

---

5 Yosiah and I wrote this song for Christmas in 2018.

You Are God and I Am Not[6]

You are God and I am not
When I am weak, you carry me safe through the storm, safe through the
    storm.
You are God and I am not,
when I fall down,
You lift me up once again, up once again.

Oh God, oh God
I'm surrounded by grace.
Oh Lord, oh Lord
You give us your strength.

> Help me to trust you're good
> Trust your love
> Trust your plans for me.
> Help me to trust your grace
> Trust your hope
> Trust you are God and I'm not.

And now I trust you're good
Trust your love
Trust your plans for me.
And now I trust your grace
Trust your hope
Trust you are God and I'm not.

---

6 I wrote this song in 2013.

Acknowledgments

I wrote in the acknowledgments of my first book that I never intended to write a book, and so I continue to be grateful to my parents for their support and ongoing encouragement to write. Even as I wrote *Beyond Our Walls*, I sensed that there needed to be a second book, as there were too many stories to fit into that first one. I also knew that my obsession with Amy Carmichael needed to be put down on paper, as the gifts I was gleaning from her life and writings were too beautiful to keep to myself. Hence, I began writing the book you are now holding.

I am very thankful for my family. For my amazing husband Yosiah who listened to my reflections about Amy Carmichael for years: you are my best friend, my soul-mate, and my partner in this journey. Words fail to express how much I love you and am grateful for you!

To my two sons, who also learned more about Amy Carmichael than most elementary-school boys would ever need to know: Mommy is so grateful for both of you! Thank you for brightening up my days and being my teachers.

I want to share just one of those bright moments. While on furlough in America, my family introduced ourselves to a neighbor as we were walking to school. "My name is Amy," the woman said.

"Amy?!?!" my seven-year-old son exclaimed in amazement and awe. "Amy Carmichael?!?" Apparently, he did not realize the name "Amy" could be used by other people!

This book was mostly written while living in the basement of my parents' house for six months. Thank you, Mom and Dad, for opening up your home, your lives, and your hearts to our noisy family. Thank you for teaching me about downward discipleship and supporting me all these years on my journey.

I am grateful also for all the churches who have invited us to share over the years and to all those who took the time to host us for dinner or tea to hear our stories. Thank you for lending a listening ear. I am also very thankful to all those who read our prayer letters and newsletters. Thank you for holding us and our dear friends in your prayers. We could not do what we do without you.

Many thanks also to those who first read this manuscript and offered valuable feedback: Jason, Katie, Chrissie, Cathy, and Carmen. And I am deeply grateful to Karen Hollenbeck Wuest, who once again has taken my rough manuscript and helped edit it into something beautiful. Thank you.

And, last, but certainly not least, I am grateful for Amy Carmichael—for her life and literary legacy that have spoken across the decades into my own heart. Thank you for taking the risk of following Jesus and for having the courage to write about it so that others might also learn from you. While I am sure that I have not portrayed your story perfectly, I pray that my haltering attempts may still be a blessing for the readers.

All praise and honor belong to the Lord Jesus. I am forever grateful to be invited on this journey of following you.

Bibliography

Carmichael, Amy. *The Beginning of a Story*. London: Morgan & Scott, 1908. Accessed in *Amy Carmichael: Her Early Works (13-in-1)*. Kindle edition.

Carmichael, Amy. *Candles in the Dark: Letters of Amy Carmichael*. First published 1981 by Dohnavur Fellowship. Fort Washington: CLC, 1999.

Carmichael, Amy. *The Continuation of a Story*. London: Dohnavur Fellowship, 1914. Accessed in *Amy Carmichael: Her Early Works (13-in-1)*. Kindle edition.

Carmichael, Amy. *From the Fight*. London: Church of England Zenana Missionary Society, 1900. Accessed in *Amy Carmichael: Her Early Works (13-in-1)*. Kindle edition.

Carmichael, Amy. *From the Forest*. London: Oliphants, 1920. Accessed in *Amy Carmichael: Her Early Works (13-in-1)*. Kindle edition.

Carmichael, Amy. *From Sunrise Land: Letters from Japan*. London: Marshall Brothers, 1895. Accessed in *Amy Carmichael: Her Early Works (13-in-1)*. Kindle edition.

Carmichael, Amy. *God's Missionary*. Fort Washington: CLC, 2002. First published 1939 by SPCK (London).

Carmichael, Amy. *Gold by Moonlight*. Fort Washington: CLC, 2020. First published 1935 by SPCK (London).

Carmichael, Amy. *Gold Cord: The Story of a Fellowship*. Fort Washington: CLC, 2002. First published 1932 by SPCK (London).

Carmichael, Amy. *If: What Do I Know of Calvary Love*. Fort Washington: CLC, 2011. First published 1938 by SPCK (London).

Carmichael, Amy. *Kohila: The Shaping of an Indian Nurse*. Madurai, India: Dohnavur Fellowship, 1939/2001.

Carmichael, Amy. *Lotus Buds*. London: Morgan & Scott, 1909. Accessed in *Amy Carmichael: Her Early Works (13-in-1)*. Kindle edition.

Carmichael, Amy. *Made in the Pans*. London: Oliphants, 1917. Accessed in *Amy Carmichael: Her Early Works (13-in-1)*. Kindle edition.

Carmichael, Amy. *Mimosa: A True Story*. Fort Washington: CLC, 2011. First published 1924 by SPCK (London). Kindle edition.

Carmichael, Amy. *Nor Scrip*. London: SPCK, 1921. Accessed in *Amy Carmichael: Her Early Works (13-in-1)*. Kindle edition.

Carmichael, Amy. *Overweights of Joy*. London: Morgan & Scott, 1906. Accessed in *Amy Carmichael: Her Early Works (13-in-1)*. Kindle edition.

Carmichael, Amy. *Plowed Under: A Young Girl's Obedience. God's Ever-Present Grace*. Fort Washington: CLC, 2013. First published 1934 by SPCK (London).

Carmichael, Amy. *Ponnamal: Her Story*. Madras, India: Diocesan Press, 1918. Accessed in *Amy Carmichael: Her Early Works (13-in-1)*. Kindle edition.

Carmichael, Amy. *Ragland Pioneer*. London: SPCK, 1922. Accessed in *Amy Carmichael: Her Early Works (13-in-1)*. Kindle edition.

Carmichael, Amy. *Rose from Brier*. Fort Washington: CLC, 2012. First published 1933 by SPCK (London).

Carmichael, Amy. *Tables in the Wilderness*. Madras, India: SPCK depository, 1923. Accessed in *Amy Carmichael Collection (7-in-1)*, vol. 2. Kindle.

Carmichael, Amy. *Things as They Are: Mission Work in Southern India*. London: Morgan and Scott, 1905. Accessed in *Amy Carmichael: Her Early Works (13-in-1)*. Kindle edition.

Carmichael, Amy. *Though the Mountains Shake*. New York: Loizeaux Brothers, 1946. First published in 1943.

Carmichael, Amy. *Toward Jerusalem*. Fort Washington: CLC, 2003. First published in 1936 by SPCK (London).

Carmichael, Amy. *Walker of Tinnevelly*. London: Morgan & Scott, 1916. Accessed in *Amy Carmichael: Her Early Works (13-in-1)*. Kindle edition.

Carmichael, Amy. *The Widow of the Jewels*. London: SPCK, 1950. First published in 1928.

Carmichael, Amy. *Windows*. London: SPCK, 1947. First published in 1937.

Dixon, Rob. "Women in the World Mission: The Untold Story." Urbana 2015. https://urbana.org/seminar/women-world-mission-untold-story.

Elliot, Elisabeth. *A Chance to Die: The Life and Legacy of Amy Carmichael*. Grand Rapids: Revell, 1987.

Greenfield, Craig. *Subversive Mission: Serving as Outsiders in a World of Need*. Downers Grove, IL: InterVarsity Press, 2022.

Hayes, John. "Incarnational Ministry in Four Dimensions." Horizon Line website. Accessed 16 January 2023. https://ic-horizonline.com/phase-1-preparing-the-laborers/incarnational-ministry-in-four-dimensions/

Heroes of the Faith. "Amy Carmichael. Mother to the Motherless." Documentary. Directed by Robert Fernandez, 2011.

Kommers, J. (Hans). *Triumphant Love: The Contextual, Creative and Strategic Missionary Work of Amy Beatrice Carmichael in South India.* South Africa: AOSIS, 2017. Kindle.

Oliver, Hillary, and Rick Green. "The Story of Amy Carmichael and the Dohnavur Fellowship (2005)." YouTube. Accessed 18 November 2020. https://www.youtube.com/watch?v=IC0UUarHU7o

Rahma, Anita. *Beyond Our Walls: Finding Jesus in the Slums of Jakarta.* Littleton, CO: William Carey Publishing, 2022.

Sangadji, Ruslan. "Central Sulawesi Disasters Killed 4,340 people, Final Count Reveals." ReliefWeb, 31 January 2019. https://reliefweb.int/report/indonesia/central-sulawesi-disasters-killed-4340-people-final-count-reveals.

Welcome Evangelical Church. "Amy Carmichael Centre: Everyone Is Welcome at the Welcome." https://welcomechurch.co.uk/amy-carmichael-centre/, accessed 23 February 2023.

WILLIAM
CAREY
PUBLISHING
visit us at missionbooks.org

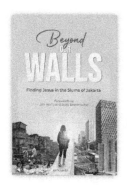

Beyond Our Walls: Finding Jesus in the Slums of Jakarta

By Anita Rahma

Beyond Our Walls provides a unique window into what ministry in an urban slum setting can look like. The author shares the amazing story of God's faithfulness in her life, as she follows Jesus into the slums of Jakarta, Indonesia, and still lives there twelve years later with her husband and two young sons. Not only have her Muslim neighbors had an opportunity to get to know a follower of Jesus, but the author herself has been forever changed by her experiences.

Facing Fear: The Journey to Mature Courage in Risk and Persecution

By Anna Hampton

Facing Fear is a practical guide for Christ-followers who long to have bold, mature courage. Cultivating this courage is necessary to endure wisely for Christ's sake. Learning to face our fears, name them, and manage them requires learning specific steps to reduce their impact on us. You'll gain valuable skills to become "shrewd as a serpent" and stand with unshaken faith in dangerous situations.

Facing Danger: A Guide Through Risk (Second Edition)

By Anna Hampton

Against the rich backdrop of her family's own sojourn in perilous places, Anna Hampton presents a treasure trove of practical tools and profound insights to help you thrive in an increasingly hazardous world. With deep spiritual contemplation and meticulous research, she offers a unique viewpoint on cross-cultural service and the art of making sacrifices.

Printed in the USA
CPSIA information can be obtained
at www.ICGtesting.com
LVHW021803120324
774228LV00005B/428